DAVID

DAVID

MARIE ROTHENBERG
and Mel White

KINGSWAY PUBLICATIONS
EASTBOURNE

ISBN 0 86065 416 8

Front cover design: Vic Mitchell

Printed in Great Britain for
KINGSWAY PUBLICATIONS LTD
Lottbridge Drove, Eastbourne, E. Sussex BN23 6NT by
Cox & Wyman Ltd, Reading.

TO David,
whose courage, determination, and
love keep my faith strong

Many of the people involved in helping David and me over-come our tragedy are mentioned in the story: my brother and sisters, John Cirillo, the Curtis family, the Buena Park Police Department, and the fine medical staff both at the University of California at Irvine Burn Center and Shriners Burns Institute of Boston.

There are other close friends too numerous to mention and thousands of people throughout the United States and Canada who joined together spiritually in their prayers to help pull David through.

Sincere thanks and gratitude to my new friend and coauthor Dr. Mel White, who not only helped me write the story but also shared many days helping me with David's treatments so he could understand more fully the pressures we were up against.

In writing David's story I hope to make more people aware of the tremendous amount of pain and suffering David and other burn victims have to face in order to survive. They are to be admired and respected for their endeavor to overlook the unwillingness of society to accept them because they look different.

1

Tuesday, February 22, 1983, began as every working day begins for me. There were no clues that a week-long countdown had begun on a crime that would change my life and the life of my son, David, forever. I stood below Carroll Street just behind the yellow line painted on the ice-cold subway station floor. I waited for that ominous rumble that signaled the approach of the F train speeding toward us beneath the streets of Brooklyn. Brakes squealed. Doors slid open. With a crowd of my commuting neighbors, I quickly stepped across the line into the graffiti-stained cars. Doors slid closed. Hands grasped poles and railings. A heavily accented conductor's voice announced something over the PA system no one could understand or has ever understood. The train jerked forward. Passengers were jostled together. No one spoke on our hectic ride beneath the East River, past lower Wall Street and Greenwich Village on our journey to my Madison Avenue stop in midtown Manhattan.

In the elevator en route to my third-floor office at an international architectural firm where I am a secretary, I began to remove the clumsy mittens that keep out subway cold. I had delivered my six-year-old son to Public School 58, just one half block from our third-floor apartment over Court Street. I was running late. There were phone calls to be made, letters to be typed, correspondence to be filed, copies to be run, and coffee to be delivered. About noon, the phone rang one more time. It was my ex-husband, Charles, calling. There was nothing unusual about his request that day, yet I felt uneasy from the moment I heard his voice.

"Marie, I'm changing jobs next week. I have six days off before I go to work for the car service in Carroll Gardens. I want to spend that time with Davie."

Charles and I had been divorced almost five years. Seldom in all that time had I refused him a visit with his son. A few times he had wanted to take David when David or his school had other important plans, but almost without exception, Charles could see his son where and when he wanted.

Charles lived six blocks from my apartment on Court Street in Brooklyn. He moved there to be near our son. On visitation days, I could trust Charles to deliver David to PS 58 and to pick him up from the day-care center when Charles finished work. On those days when my ex-husband had our son, I would see them in the park near Davie's school, in the grocery store, or at the video-game mart. Often we would meet at Helen's Italian Restaurant for dinner or I would invite Charles to the apartment for Chinese food or pizza. There was no reason to suspect that this visit would be any different from the others. Yet the next night, when Charles came for Davie, I began to feel afraid.

"Look at this brand-new suitcase, Davie," Charles said, entering my apartment with a large piece of luggage in his hand. "You can forget the shopping bag this visit," he added.

David was ecstatic. He loved those times with his father. Why shouldn't he? From the day David was born, Charles was a proud, possessive, and overindulgent father. Charles had told me he had been raised in an orphanage in upstate New York. He wanted to be the kind of father he himself had never had, or so he said. When David was born, Charles filled my room with five different arrangements of carnations.

"Thank you for my son, Marie," he whispered in my ear a dozen times during the four days I was in the hospital.

The day David was born, Charles rushed about Brooklyn buying a special bassinet for the child and filling it with gifts and clothing. For the next two years he carried Davie up and down the neighborhood bragging to friends and strangers alike about the beauty and brilliance of his son.

Charles worked as a waiter between twelve and fourteen hours a day. He was home only one day a week. That day he devoted entirely to his son. He regularly took David shopping and bought him fifty or sixty dollars' worth of toys, until our apartment was cluttered with enough games, puzzles, and toys to stock a store.

"My son, my son," Charles would say, over and over again. "Look at my beautiful son."

At first friends and neighbors thought it was wonderful to see a father so adoring of his child. But there was a dark side to that love, even then. Day by day Charles' preoccupation with David became a stronger and stronger obsession. Charles refused to let his child cry. He did anything to keep his son happy. As a result, in those first two years of his life David became almost unmanageable. His father indulged his every whim. There was nothing David wanted that he couldn't have. There was nothing Davie wanted to do that his father wouldn't permit. And when I tried to step in to discipline the two-year-old, Charles became enraged. He warned me not to ever let his baby cry, and I knew his threat was real.

One night just before his second birthday, David refused to go to bed. It was late. I picked him up from the pile of new toys his dad had given him, and placed him in his bed. David had a tantrum. In spite of Charles' warnings, I let him cry. I stood beside David's bed, rubbing his back, trying to calm him with a nursery song I'd learned from my own childhood. David continued to cry and I knew it was time to let him cry one out. Suddenly the door flew open. Charles had returned from work early. He heard the baby crying. My husband rushed across the room and threw me up against a wall. He picked up David in his arms, sat down in the rocking chair, and rocked him for more than an hour until David finally went to sleep.

I was young. David was my first child. No one taught me how to care for him. But I knew I couldn't give in to his tears. I hated to hear him crying but I knew it was worse in the long run to let him control me with those baby tears. Our landlady, who had raised her own family, agreed with me.

"Let him cry himself to sleep," she advised. "Then he'll learn that you are the parent and he is the child."

So this time I tried it, and my husband threw me up against the wall. I sneaked from the room, feeling hurt and frightened. I fixed myself a cup of tea and was sitting on the sofa drinking it when Charles closed David's door and ran toward me across the room.

"I told you not to let my baby cry," he reminded me, flinging the cup of tea across the carpet. He grabbed me by the neck and ripped off my nightgown. He knocked me to the floor and started kicking me. I screamed for help. A neighbor called the police. Our landlady tried to reason with my husband.

"You must let him cry, Charles, or you will spoil him." But Charles would not hear of it.

We were divorced not long after that, and though I had good reason to be afraid of Charles' violent side, I had absolutely no reason to fear that he would harm our son. Quite to the contrary, after our divorce Charles continued to indulge David. He had complete visitation rights to our son and often they would return with an armload of toys. Charles installed a tape answering service in his apartment so that "I will never have to miss a call from my son." He even wore a beeper so that David could contact his daddy any time of the day or night. The neighbors and David's principal and teachers at PS 58 and the day-care center saw Charles as the perfect father. There was absolutely no reason I should feel afraid for David that day Charles came to pick up our six-year-old for a week-long visit.

And though there were clues that left me uneasy, the reasons were not enough to make me cancel the visit. Charles arrived at my apartment Wednesday night wearing a new plaid shirt and designer jeans. He looked wonderful. He was genuinely happy to see us and excited about having Davie for the weekend. David rushed about the room in a flurry, glad to be going with his dad.

"I'll get my Atari tapes, Daddy. We'll fill up your new suitcase with them."

Charles laughed. "We won't need Atari this time, David. We're going to the country for the weekend to a game farm in the Catskills."

Not need tapes? David loved to play his collection of Atari video games with his father. Any visit of more than one day with his dad without those tapes would have been a mistake. They were going to be at Charles' apartment for the entire time, I thought, except for the weekend. Why would Charles discourage Davie from bringing those tapes?

And the Catskills, in the winter? I should have known it was a lie, but again I missed the clue.

"And we'll need at least two pair of shoes, Marie," Charles requested.

"Why extra shoes?" I asked. "I'm right next door. If you need more shoes or extra clothing, you can get them. I'll even bring them over."

"Get me the shoes, Marie."

Needing extra shoes was strange enough, but the rude and demanding way Charles ordered me to get them was another clue I missed.

"There's going to be a special assembly at David's school on Friday," I said to Charles. "He'll need his red tie."

"I have a red tie, Marie," Charles interrupted impatiently. "He can wear mine."

My uneasiness was growing. Before I could get David's school clothes and books together, Charles and David were headed toward the door, hand in hand.

"Good-bye, Davie," I called out to my son. "How about a kiss for Mommy?"

David squirmed around impatiently as they headed for the door.

"Not now, Mommy. I want to be with Daddy."

Then they were gone. How many times they had walked out that door together and I had felt relief. A single working parent needs some time alone, but that night I didn't feel relief. I felt a growing sense of alarm.

The next day, I called Charles at his apartment to get his order for Easter candy the school was selling. I suppose I was only using the candy sale as an excuse to see how Charles and David were doing on their week-long visit. But there was no reply. Several times during the evening I called. Still no answer. I left messages on the answering machine. I assumed Charles had taken David out to dinner or a movie or shopping or to visit Charles' girl friend. When I called my fiancé, John Cirillo, a policeman, to share my growing anxiety, he kidded me and reminded me that Charles had never really given me cause to worry about David.

"He loves him, Marie. He'll take care of him. You know that."

Friday Charles called.

"You will pick David up from day care after school on Wednesday, won't you Marie?"

"Of course," I answered. It seemed a strange reminder, out of place somehow. Surely I would see them before Wednesday. Even if they went to the Catskills for the weekend, I would see them on Monday or Tuesday. Surely we would at least talk on the phone before Wednesday. Looking back now I realize that Charles was trying to distance me for the week. He hoped that I would just forget my son until that Wednesday afternoon five days hence. It didn't work. That strange comment only made me more determined to follow every movement Charles made with our son during that visit.

Saturday, John and I drove to New Jersey to visit a famous flea market there. I spent the day bothering him with my suspicions.

"Why are you worried, Marie?" he asked. "What did Charles say that upset you?"

"I know that man," I answered. "I've seen that look in his eyes before."

"Well, call them," John advised. "See what they're doing today. Maybe then you'll relax."

"I can't call them," I answered. "They're at a game farm in the Catskills."

John looked surprised. "He can't be at a game farm in the Catskills," he said. "It's February. That's a summertime operation. It's too cold up there now. The whole area closes down for the winter."

We called Charles' apartment all weekend and early Monday morning. There was no reply. I invented all kinds of excuses for their absence. They *had* gone to the Catskills to a place that *was* open and there *were* no phones. At the last minute Charles had discovered the resort closed and took David somewhere else on a weekend holiday. Charles would deliver Davie to school Monday morning directly from their weekend together. Then he would return to the apartment, get my messages, and return my calls at work. Frankly, with all the reasonable excuses I could find, I still choked down a terrible, growing fear that my son had been kidnapped by his father and that I might not see him again.

All day Monday I called Charles' apartment from my office phone. Monday night I called his number again and again. At 10:30 Monday night I called a neighbor whose child was in David's class.

"Hello, Ruthlynn. This is Marie, Davie's mom. Forgive me for bothering you at night with such a strange question, but I need your help."

"What's wrong, Marie?" she asked.

"Will you ask Christopher if Davie was in school today?"

"Sure. He's in bed, but I'll ask him."

I could hear their conversation in the background.

"Chris, was David Rothenberg in school today?"

"No, Mommy. Mrs. Klapper was asking has anybody seen David because he's not been in school."

My anxiety turned to terror.

"Ruthlynn," I yelled into the phone.

She picked up the receiver.

"Ask Christopher if Davie was in school Friday."

"I don't think so," I heard him answer from his bedroom.

"Ask him if he was there on Thursday," I said, practically hysterical.

"I don't remember, Mommy."

"Please, try to remember," I begged.

"He can't remember, Marie. I'm sorry. What's happened?"

"Later . . . please, I'll explain later."

It took me three tries to get the phone back into its cradle. I assumed that David would be in school on Thursday and Friday as Charles had promised. But I hadn't called the school. I had called Charles' apartment again and again on the weekend and all day Monday, but I hadn't called the school. I felt angry and stupid and irresponsible.

I called John at his apartment. "Charles has kidnapped David," I told him. "I can't find either one of them."

"Try to be calm, Marie," he answered. He had sixteen years of police experience with cases like my own. "Call where Charles works. See if he's been there. Maybe they will know."

"Luchow's. May I help you?" A receptionist answered at the fashionable eatery in Manhattan. Charles had worked there as a waiter for the past eight months.

"I would like to speak with someone about an ex-employee," I said, remembering that Charles had told me he was changing jobs the following Wednesday.

"What is the person's name?" the receptionist asked.

"Charles Rothenberg," I answered.

There was a long, awkward pause.

"One moment, please. I will switch you to our manager."

How often I had sensed the same embarrassing silence after mentioning Charles' name to an employer or a former employer. Charles never had trouble getting a job. He is a handsome man. He knew what to say and when to say it. People were drawn to him. He had a long criminal record but no one, including myself, even thought to ask about his past.

We had been married about a month when I first learned that Charles was a criminal. I married a man who was wanted by the FBI for forging a twenty-three-thousand-dollar check against his ex-employer in San Francisco, and I didn't even know it. It wasn't his first crime. People wonder why I got mixed up with that man. It isn't easy to explain.

He was charming. The first day we met on Montague Street in Brooklyn he handed me a rose. A flow of gifts and cards and words of love quickly followed. I fell for him. I was alone in the city. My father was dead. My mother and stepmother had both beaten me as a child. When I was just a teenager I moved from Pennsylvania to New York

City to escape their abuse. I struggled to survive and I made it on my own, but I was lonely. Charles seemed to love me. When he moved to San Francisco he begged me to follow him there. So, I quit my job. I left my friends and my apartment in the City and, like a fool, I followed. Just as I was finding new friends, a new job, and a new place to live, he moved back to New York. And one more time I followed him.

Charles was intense, irresponsible, and unpredictable, given to moods and bursts of violent temper, but he seemed to love me. I didn't dream he was running from the police. I had no one else. So I took the risk. We were married in a dark, gray, gloomy civil court in Brooklyn. There were no witnesses, no flowers, no rice. He had bought a Laundromat in Brooklyn with the money he said he had "earned" in San Francisco. We worked hard to make our business a success. The money he spent on the Laundromat was the money the FBI was looking for. Charles called me from the city jail thirty days after we were married. An FBI agent told me, "Do yourself a favor. Leave this guy. He is no good. Get as far away from this man as you possibly can." I should have listened.

When Charles was arraigned at New York's Municipal Court Building he cried and begged me not to leave him. My family advised me to "give Charles another chance." My friends said, "Stand by him. He needs you." So against my own better judgment, I stayed.

After nine months' imprisonment in California, Charles was transferred by the courts to a work-furlough program in San Francisco. I visited him there. I returned to New York not knowing that our son, David, had been conceived. Three months later Charles was released from prison.

As I waited for the manager of Luchow's to pick up the phone I grew more and more afraid that he would tell me Charles was wanted by the police again.

"Can I help you?" the manager asked.

"I'm looking for my ex-husband, Charles Rothenberg." I tried to sound calm, but failed. "Do you know where he might be? Does anyone there know?"

"Mrs. Rothenberg, if we knew where he was we would feel a lot better. We've had the police issue a warrant for his arrest. If you find out where he's gone, please tell us."

Charles had been fired for alleged misconduct, probably theft. In apparent retaliation he had gained entry into Luchow's computer room after working hours. He had spray-painted the valuable computer and written graffiti on the restaurant walls. The news was terrifying. Charles was not just taking David on a holiday. Charles was trying to escape the police again; only this time he had taken David with him. I had no idea where they were or how to find them.

I had one last hope. Charles told me he would begin work on Thursday with Larry Kanterwitz at the nearby car service on Court Street. I found Larry's number and called him, hoping that I had just been imagining everything.

"Larry, I need your help. Charles told me he's going to work for you this week. Is it true?"

I held my breath. *Please, God, let this be a bad dream.*

"Work for me?" Larry answered with surprise. "I haven't seen Charles in a long time. He's giving you a snow job, Marie."

At that moment my worst fears were proven true. I dialed my brother-in-law.

"Charles has kidnapped David," I cried out to him.

"What?" he exclaimed.

"Can you come right now and help me look through Charles' apartment?"

"I'll be right there, Marie. Hang on."

We drove the six blocks to Huntington Street. I ran across the ragged strip of grass, bounded up the short flight of stairs, and pressed Charles' doorbell. There was no response. I ran to the landlord's apartment. He wasn't in, either. Finally we roused a neighbor lady.

"Have you seen my ex-husband, Charles Rothenberg?" I asked her. "He's kidnapped my baby."

"If I had only known sooner," she replied, running up to me. "If I had known where to find you. That man is crazy," she continued. "He's gone. I saw him leaving with his suitcase last Thursday."

"Thursday!" I exclaimed. "Was David with him?"

"No," she replied. "He was alone. He was rushing around here like a madman, dumping things in the trash over there."

"What kind of things?" I asked her.

"Pictures," she said "of your son. They were cut or torn into pieces. And there were personal bills and even his apartment lease. That man's no good, you know. He stole checks from my mailbox but wouldn't admit it. Said they never came. I know a—"

"May I use your phone to call the police?" I interrupted.

A squad car arrived almost immediately. Two patrolmen got out and walked over to us. "My son has been missing for five days," I said. "The neighbor here saw my ex-husband leave this apartment with his suitcase four days ago. I think my child is inside that place. You've got to go in and find him."

The policemen told me they couldn't enter the apartment without a search warrant. I was hysterical. They tried to explain. I cried and insisted they look for Davie. Finally, they took the risk. The landlord had arrived and provided a key. Just as we went through the front door, one of the policemen noticed a note taped to the door frame. Charles had written that he had gone to "upstate New York for one month." Inside on the kitchen table there was another note addressed to his landlord.

"Thanks for everything," it read. "Here are your keys. I will not be returning. Charles Rothenberg."

Except for David's bike and a few old toys, the apartment was empty. "He took my baby," I sobbed. "He took my baby."

The police searched the apartment, hoping not to find the body of my son. Then we drove to the station house to file a missing-person report.

"Mrs. Rothenberg, you must go through the family court," a duty officer explained. "There are channels for this kind of misunderstanding. . . ."

"This is not a misunderstanding," I told him. "And I will not go through the family court. My husband is crazy. I don't want my son alone with him one more day. I want a detective assigned to this case and I want you to use every trick you have to find him."

The police were caught off guard by the fury of my attack. They agreed to bypass the family court. They assigned a detective to the case and put out an all-points bulletin describing Charles and David.

By their rules and regulations, they shouldn't have taken the case. But they did and I am grateful.

Monday night I waited for a call. There was none. Tuesday morning I took the F train from Carroll Station to my office in Manhattan. Charles knew my number at work. If he did call, he would try there first. Besides, I decided, the police were doing all they could to find David. I might as well be working instead of sitting idly in the apartment waiting for his call. In the meantime there was nothing I could do but wait and worry.

Just before lunch, Charles called.

"Hi, Marie," he said calmly.

Words rushed out of me. "Charles, where are you? What have you done with David? Let me talk to him."

"You can't, Marie," he answered slowly.

"Why not?" I shouted into the phone.

"He's sleeping," Charles mumbled, intimidated, I'm afraid, by my loud, angry questions.

"Why is he still asleep?" I continued. "It's almost lunchtime."

"It's the time dif—" he began to answer. Then he was silent.

"What about the time?" I asked, confused, trying to get him to finish his statement. "Where are you?"

Then I remembered Charles asked to take David out of school for a trip to Disney World. I had refused. But there is no time difference between New York and Florida.

"Are you in California?" I asked, pleading for information. "Are you visiting Disneyland?" There would be a three-hour time difference if he had gone to California. David could be sleeping. In all probability Charles had taken David to the West Coast to escape his troubles with Luchow's and to indulge his son one more time before the police caught him and hauled him back to face the courts again.

"Are you at Disneyland?" I asked again, straining to remain calm.

"No, Marie, of course not," he answered. "I tried to get reservations for California but I couldn't. I'm in upstate New York," he insisted. "I'm on a farm where no one can find me."

I knew he was lying but I was desperate. I was afraid he would hang up. I wanted some clue.

"Please, let me talk to Davie," I begged him.

He refused. "No, he's fine Marie. He's sleeping. You can talk to him later."

The line went dead. The dial tone buzzed loudly in my ear. I was almost sure that they were in California.

About fifteen minutes later, Charles called again.

"David wants to talk to you, Marie, but he's busy right now."

His voice was drained of energy. I could picture him standing with his neck bent, his head down, cradling the phone with both hands, trying to keep Davie from hearing the call.

"Charles, where are you?"

I could hear the sounds of video games in the background, the kinds of games you play in an arcade or a hotel game room.

"Charles, let me talk to David."

"He can't talk now, Marie," Charles answered.

"Why?" I shouted into the phone.

Charles paused. "He's playing a video game."

"Interrupt the game," I demanded angrily. "Give him another quarter. He can play again later. Put him on the phone."

There was silence.

"I'm going to keep him for a while, Marie," he said.

We argued. I begged. Charles refused. I don't remember exactly how the conversation finished that day. In an interview with the *Los Angeles Times* quoted around the world by the Associated Press and United Press International, Charles said that I threatened he would never see his son again after they returned to Brooklyn.

I don't remember saying that, but I was close to hysteria and might have made just such a threat. I hope I didn't say it. Charles blamed that threat of mine, real or imagined, as the reason he tried to murder our son.

When Charles hung up the phone I notified the police. I told them he had promised to call that night at 7:00 P.M. They carefully instructed me how to respond to Charles if he called again. "Promise anything," they said. "Stay calm. Keep Charles calm. Listen for clues. Find out where he is. Talk to David." But it was too late. Charles didn't call that night as he had promised.

There was no word on Wednesday, either. I grew more frantic by the hour. The police were doing all they could. Word spread around the office. It seemed that everyone was waiting for some news about David. Finally, on Thursday, my phone rang. I took a deep breath and answered.

"Hello?"

There was a brief silence and then the phone went dead. Quickly, I called our operator.

"Was it Charles?" I asked.

"Yes, Marie, but just as I connected him, the line went dead."

Again we waited. Twenty minutes later, the phone rang again. It wasn't Charles. A Western Union operator spoke softly, her voice trembling.

"Mrs. Rothenberg?"

"Yes," I answered. "What is it?"

"I have a telegram for you. May I read it?" She sounded as though she was about to cry.

My stomach knotted. My palms grew damp. I was trembling and ready to cry myself.

"Yes," I whispered. "Read it."

"Dear Marie," the operator began. "By the time you read this I will have terminated my existence."

My heart stopped. Charles had never threatened suicide before. Was he playing some kind of trick? What had happened to David? The operator's voice was filled with grief.

"You have caused me enough harm," continued the sympathetic operator. "I've gone through enough."

Harm? Charles, what harm have I caused you? I screamed silently as the voice continued echoing Charles' words. "What are you saying? What has happened to my son?"

"Also be informed," the operator read quietly, "that your son has been in an accident and is in the University of California at Irvine Medical Center Burn Center."

Two telephone numbers followed.

Hysterical, I wrote down the numbers and dropped the phone. Friends and fellow workers had gathered around the open door to my office. Walter Oerlemans, the personnel manager of the firm, helped me to a chair. For a moment I froze, fighting back the tears. Then I lunged for the phone, dialing the first number Charles' telegram had listed.

An operator at the University of California at Irvine Medical Center Burn Center answered my call. Immediately I was transferred to Detective Alice Lauter of the Buena Park Police Department.

"I am searching for my child," I cried. "His name is David Rothenberg. I just received a telegram from his father stating that David was in an accident. Tell me. What has happened to my son?"

2

Detective Alice Lauter could not tell me how or why David had been burned. She didn't know. Only Charles knew how and why we had been plunged into this nightmare. But Charles had vanished from the motel near Disneyland, leaving the Buena Park Police Department to answer my questions.

The manager at Luchow's Restaurant had provided the first disturbing clue. There was a warrant out for Charles' arrest. He was not simply a divorced father out on a field day with our child. He was a man with a long criminal record who was on the run again. Only this time he had our six-year-old son. Charles knew he could not return to Brooklyn without risking arrest.

Charles' current girl friend provided a second clue. The Friday night before Charles and David flew to California, she had dined with them in Helen's Restaurant, less than half a block north of my apartment on Court Street.

There are no McDonalds in our old Italian neighborhood in Brooklyn. Carroll Gardens has no Taco Bell, no Colonel Sanders, no Baskin and Robbins. But there is a Helen's Italian Restaurant, with five red Naugahyde booths, a scattering of tables covered in starchy white tablecloths, a long rack for winter coats and scarves, and a tiny kitchen presided over by seventy-two-year-old Helen herself. Charles and I have eaten regularly at Helen's for more than five years.

That Friday, even Helen remembered how anxious Charles

seemed. Charles, his girl friend, and David entered the restaurant and ordered the special. While the meal was being prepared, father and son began to yell at each other angrily.

"You little brat!" Charles screamed at David.

Like his mother, our son is neither timid nor passive. According to eyewitnesses, David yelled back at his father. Charles shoved the child with his shoulder, forcing David to his knees on the restaurant floor. David began to cry.

"Shut up," Charles warned him. "I'm sending you home to your mother."

It was the first time Charles' girl friend remembered his striking our son. I don't think Charles ever hit David before. Looking back, it was another clue as to the emotional state of Charles just days before he tried to kill David. No one intervened. I was less than a block away, yet no one thought to call me and report the incident.

Airline records offer a third clue. The next day (at 10:00 A.M.) Charles and David flew to California, probably on a TWA flight from La Guardia. They took a limousine to the Buena Park Holiday Inn near Disneyland and checked into the hotel at 2:30 P.M. It was raining.

Apparently, when it rains in Southern California for any length of time, everything stops. The freeways are coated with a thin film of oil and gas that causes cars to float or hydroplane across the surface without traction. Accidents tie up freeways. Water collects in intersections and parking lots. Underpasses and cross streets are flash flooded. When it rains, everybody who is able stays at home and the cities close down. Tourist attractions know that the flow of visitors will slow if not stop altogether. Disneyland was the first to close its gates that day. Knott's Berry Farm stayed open to get the extra business, then it, too, closed down. Magic Mountain, like the other open-air theme parks in the greater Los Angeles area, finally turned off its lights. All the attractions that Charles had promised David closed up when it began to rain and stayed closed for five long days.

David and his very nervous father were locked up in that motel room from Saturday, February 26, until March 2. There are some clues as to how they spent their time. Charles paid twenty dollars each for two temporary memberships at Wallbangers, a health club with handball courts, aerobics programs, and video games. Charles rented a car and apparently tried to keep his promise to take Davie to the beach. Nothing worked and the rain continued falling.

It is not difficult to imagine what was happening to my ex-husband

and our son as they sat, day after day, in that Holiday Inn room watching the rain wash out their California fantasy. Charles had always overindulged our son. It was the only way he knew to win Davie's favor. Charles fought hard to keep David's love and loyalty by spoiling him with gifts and surprises. He must have promised our son everything on this last Disneyland fling, but the rain continued falling and Charles could not deliver on his promises.

David was only six. Disneyland was just outside the window, Knott's Berry Farm minutes away. The beaches were down the road a bit. He must have grown more and more bored, more and more restless.

You have to understand our neighborhood in Brooklyn to really understand the excitement of Southern California and how frustrating the weather must have been to David. David grew up in Carroll Gardens, Brooklyn. Our third-floor apartment looked down on Carroll Park. On three sides of that square block park are old, three-story, turn-of-the-century houses now turned into apartments. On the fourth side is Public School 58, a yellow, three-story, cement-block building. In the middle of the park is a flagpole with two statues facing it. One honors the sailors from Brooklyn who lost their lives in World War II. The other, a doughboy, honors the soldiers who "sought for glory by dying for their country's good." Spray-paint graffiti covers the soldier and the sailor and the long list of names of those boys from Carroll Gardens who died. Graffiti covers the cement-block rest rooms, the sidewalks, the trash containers. Even the tall, stark, maple trees have occasional graffiti sprayed on trunk and limb. In the winter mothers push earmuffed babies in prams through the park. Neighborhood boys play rough games or roller hockey. Italian men smoke cigarillos, play bocci ball, and gossip in Italian dialects about the old country. And in the summer the gray sycamore trees regain their leaves and shade the cement wading pool, the rusty slides, swings, and teeter-totters.

In the daylight, Carroll Park is a wonderful though graffiti-stained oasis; at night the same park becomes dark and formidable. Leaving the Carroll Street subway station, commuters avoid the park or rush past on the far side of Smith or President Streets. The few street lights cast eerie shadows over neighborhood youths clustered in the darkness. These are not bad kids. They have no other place to gather and in the early evening they dance to the heavy beat of radios or shoot baskets by moonlight. Later on, kids preside over Carroll Park and we close our windows and lock our doors against the moving shadows, the whispered silence, and the sudden violent sights and sounds that sometimes scar the night.

David grew up in Carroll Park. Like his friends, he dreamed of Disneyland, of clean, wide streets, of graffiti-free, freshly painted buildings, of marching bands in clean white tunics and flaming red pants, of popcorn and hot dogs, of fireworks and safe, brightly lit streets. To fly across the nation with his father, to move into the Buena Park Holiday Inn, to wake up on that first Disneyland day and then to drive up to the park and find it closed must have been an awful shock. But to repeat that process five days in a row is unthinkable. And poor Charles: wanting to please and impress his son, knowing that the minutes were ticking away before he would be found and jailed again, sensing my anger over the phone for stealing our son away from me, feeling his own growing helplessness and his son's increasing hostility —all of this must have left Charles in a terrible emotional state.

I have gone over those days in my mind a thousand times. I have tried to find some reason good enough to excuse Charles for the crime he was about to commit. But I cannot. On Saturday my son and my ex-husband landed in Los Angeles en route to Disneyland. On Wednesday, four days later, Charles entered a hardware store in Buena Park and bought a plastic, two-and-one-half-gallon container of kerosene.

What drove Charles to think of fire that day? No one can explain it. Looking back, there is evidence that Charles often thought of fire as a way to vent his anger. A mysterious fire almost destroyed our second Laundromat just when Charles realized he had made a mistake in buying it. Charles was the only suspect in that fire, but he made a settlement with the owner of the building and escaped without any criminal prosecution. Another mysterious fire burned the three flights of stairs to my apartment after our divorce. The stairwell exploded in flames and David and I barely escaped down the outside metal stairway. At first Charles was not allowed back in our building after that fire, but again he was not arrested or tried for the crime. Then again, in Buena Park, he thought of fire to end this terrible holiday with his son.

He bought the kerosene and placed it in the trunk of a rented white Chevrolet Cavalier. He drove to a nearby motel and rented room 139. He kept his room at the Holiday Inn. He had called me from that hotel to tell me Davie wanted to come home. The video games I heard Davie playing during that phone call were in the lobby.

For the last year I have lived and relived Charles' actions that day, wondering what I could have done to stop him. I have blamed myself for his crime. In the Old Testament Solomon wrote, "A soft answer turns away wrath." If I had reasoned softly with my husband when he called that day, if I had been more sensitive to his dilemma and less consumed by my own, if I had called the police earlier to trace the phone calls, if I had been more careful, more creative in my response. If . . . if . . . if . . . .

Wednesday, March 2, David and his dad moved from the Holiday Inn to the Buena Park TraveLodge. Charles backed his car into the space near his room. The police reported his car was the only one backed into a motel parking space. During the early evening six-year-old David probably watched television, never suspecting the crime his daddy was about to commit. David didn't like getting ready for bed, but sometime during that night Charles got David into his blue pajamas and into the queen-sized bed.

During the court proceedings there was no mention of a sleeping pill, but several months ago, more than a year after our tragedy, David and I saw a television commercial featuring a sleeping aid. When David saw the brightly colored pill, his expression changed.

"What's the pill for?" he finally asked.

"That's a sleeping pill," I answered.

David was silent again, trying to remember something distant, unreal. Then he said, "Daddy gave me a pill just like that before he. . . ." David didn't finish his sentence. He saw the look of horror and disbelief in my eyes.

Charles said during his arraignment that he had planned to take his own life. But there is absolutely no evidence of that. He claimed that he lost his courage and then tried to rescue our boy. There is eyewitness evidence to the contrary. That sleeping pill was the final blow to the many excuses I had tried to make for Charles. That night in room 139 Charles Rothenberg tried to murder our son, David, and there will never be enough reasons to answer the question "Why?"

Maysal Nadine Kuhns was another guest in the TraveLodge that night. Her room was on the second floor of the east building adjacent to and above the room where Charles and David were staying. Between 11:50 P.M. and midnight, Mrs. Kuhns looked out her front west window to see if it was still raining. She saw a white car backed into the stall directly in front of room 139. She noticed it because the door on the driver's side was open and the engine was running.

At that moment, she saw Charles come out of the open motel room door. He was carrying a large white jug. She saw him walk to a trash barrel just to the right of the building and place the jug inside the barrel. Then he returned to room 139 and bent over as if to pick up something just inside the room. He stood up, closed the door, and walked quickly to the white car.

Mrs. Kuhns said he slammed the door of the white car and drove at least forty miles an hour through the parking lot toward Beach Boulevard. When the car was about halfway through the lot, she heard a loud explosion and the window of room 139 blew out. Flames came rushing through the shattered glass. She said she could hear screams coming from inside the burning room.

The sound of the explosion and of breaking glass awakened people on both sides of room 139. A man began to kick down the front door. Flames leaped out at him. Someone else ran up with a chemical fire extinguisher plucked from a nearby wall and began to spray the burning room. David's screams for help had stopped. He lay on his back on the floor at the foot of the bed, with his head and hands facing toward the open doorway.

Geoffrey Michelin, a Chicago businessman, was in Buena Park at the TraveLodge on business when David's screams and the sound of breaking glass awakened him. As he ran to the scene, two still-unidentified men were already fighting their way through the flames to drag David to safety. Twice they were beaten back by the fire. Then Michelin entered the room on his hands and knees and pulled Davie the rest of the way out of the flames.

In an interview with the *Los Angeles Times,* Michelin admitted he is still haunted by visions of the charred boy, wearing only the neck band of his pajamas as he dragged him through the flames across the melting carpet.

Fire must reach between nine hundred and one thousand degrees Fahrenheit to explode a light bulb. Three light bulbs and the television tube inside room 139 exploded from the intense heat. Witnesses say the upholstery of the chairs, the bedding, the lamp shades, the curtains, all were burned away. The synthetic carpet melted, releasing toxic fumes and fusing itself to David's back and legs.

Paramedics arrived on the scene just in time to place David gently on a stretcher. He was charred black from head to toe. His pajamas had been burned away and third-degree burns covered more than 90 percent of his body. Immediately, a paramedic placed a fluid-bearing catheter into David's arms and covered my son with blankets for the long, painful ride to the University of California at Irvine Medical Center Burn Center several miles away.

Police and paramedics radioed the hospital to prepare to receive a small, badly burned child. Immediately the night shift notified Sue Martinez, the head nurse, who put in calls for other skilled nurses and doctors to join her at the Burn Center. By the time David was rushed into the intensive-care section there were a total of fourteen skilled medical people (six doctors and at least eight nurses) waiting to receive him. They worked nonstop through the night to save my son. Looking back, the grief and failure I feel for not having been there myself to help him is compensated in large part by the fact that so many others came through for us without even being asked.

David's toes and fingers, his nose and ears, every tiny appendage had been seared through by the flames. Most of his skin had been burned away leaving blood, veins, muscles, and organs exposed and vulnerable. The nurses all remember his alert brown eyes staring up at them in pain and fear. They tried to reassure him, but they did not even know his name.

As emergency personnel worked to save my son, no one really knew who he was or why this awful thing had happened. Rumors were whispered among the hospital personnel as they passed one another in the silent corridors. A man had been seen running from the burning room. What awful act had been committed to need the evidence burned away?

Since that night I have spent more than a year in and around the intensive-care units of the UCI Burn Center and of the Shriners Children's Hospital in Boston. I have seen these wonderfully trained medical teams work to save other children brought in screaming in the middle of the night. Unfortunately, many of them who are burned less than David die as the process of resuscitation begins.

Dee Fraser, one of the nurses David and I have grown to love, remembers looking down at my son that first night and saying to herself, "There is no way this kid is going to make it." She did not reckon with David. He is a fighter and his will to survive is strong. "He cooperated with us from the very first moment of treatment," remembers Geri Chambers, another important nurse who helped save my son. "I asked him to move his arm and immediately he tried to move it."

"I hated not knowing his name," Sue Martinez, the head nurse who guided the others through David's treatment, recalls. "I called him 'sugar' or 'sweetheart' or 'honey.' When I asked him if he could hear me, he nodded yes. I said he was going to be okay and that he could help us if he would. Again, he nodded yes."

When David was admitted that night he still smelled of smoke and fumes. Melted carpet was fused to his body. He was covered with ashes and soot and dirt from the fire. Quickly, gentle hands lowered Davie into a whirlpool bath. The warm water washed away much of the refuse and some of the dead, blistered skin that still hung in folds from his limbs and torso.

I have since learned how many tasks had to be performed simultaneously that night to save David's life. He had literally swallowed flames as he lay on his back in the fire. He had gasped the dense, toxic fumes into his system. They, in turn, had seared his throat and trachea. The inner lining of his lungs had been burned away. As the swelling of the remaining live tissue began, the throat could close in on itself and strangle my son. An endotracheal tube was forced down through his mouth and throat. A ventilator forced air through the tube into David's lungs so that David would not die as the swelling closed off his airways.

The threat of infection was massive. Dead skin was sloughed off. David's body was one large, open wound. Nurses, doctors, and orderlies wore long blue gowns, masks, and sterile gloves as they worked on my child. Silvadene ointment was smoothed onto his entire body to cover the burns and ward off infection. A light, white protective netting was placed on top of the dressing. David was ghostlike and completely unrecognizable. Only his brown eyes shone up from that oozing mass of white.

Hard, synthetic catheters were inserted into David, carrying fluid and nutrients to keep his body from dehydrating. Those fluid-bearing intravenous lines must be placed in a patient within a very short time of the actual burn or the body will go into shock from loss of fluids escaping through the burned body tissues. Gallons of fluids drained into David during those first hours just to cope with his tremendous fluid loss. This was very hard on his heart, kidneys, and lungs. So all his survival systems had to be constantly monitored for emergency overloads. Another catheter was placed in David's penis to drain away the urine. Yet another tube was placed to drain his stomach so that he would not throw up. Just the stress of such a traumatic accident can cause the body to vomit and thus unstabilize the patient, who is already close to death.

David lay staring up at the doctors and nurses rushing about to save him. Almost immediately, his body began to swell. His eyelids were so swollen that they came out and turned backward on themselves. Immediate surgery was required on his eyelids. His head had been burned down to the skull and the tissue left began to swell until his head seemed the size of a basketball.

Later, the doctors explained to me that the outer skin had been burned hard as tanned leather. Just below the hard, burned tissues, the circulation system was leaking and all the combined fluids were building up. The doctors poured in more fluids to save the child and they joined in the buildup. The outer tissue would not expand because it was charred. So the increased pressure built until the body became swollen, like a balloon. All the time those other procedures were taking place to save David, doctors were making incisions in the burned areas to allow the pressure to be relieved.

Lights in panels flashed. Machines beeped and hummed. Lines darted and danced in cathode-ray tubes, all monitoring David's progress. Nurses stood in one position over David until their legs cramped and their arms ached from holding his head and body in place. One thrashing arm could tear out a life-giving intravenous tube. One involuntary shudder could cause more harm to an already overloaded system. Doctors and nurses were everywhere using everything they had learned in years of school and on-the-job experience to save my child.

At the same time police and firemen were searching through the ashes and interviewing every eyewitness to learn how and why the child had been burned. Charles had disappeared and the Buena Park police launched a nationwide manhunt to find him.

At that very moment, Charles sent the telegram that informed me of David's accident, checked out of the Holiday Inn, drove his rented car to the airport, returned it, and bought a ticket to San Francisco. He listed his name as David Love.

3

While Dr. Bruce Achauer and his team in the Burn Center at UCI intensive care were working to save a six- or seven-year-old "John Doe," friends and co-workers filled my tiny Manhattan office. They listened as I spoke on the telephone to Detective Alice Lauter of the Buena Park, California, Police Department, on duty at the Burn Center.

"Yes, we have an unidentified child here, Mrs. Rothenberg."

"Is it David?"

"We don't know."

"Why don't you know? Can't you ask him? Ask his father."

"The child is alone, Mrs. Rothenberg. Did you say your missing child is six years old and that his name is David?"

"Yes, David. Davie."

"One moment, please."

There was silence. I did not understand why the detective seemed so dense. If there was a child there, why didn't she just ask him his name? My hands shook. The office grew silent. I waited an eternity, never dreaming the condition of the child lying in that bed three thousand miles away. I believed with all my heart it was not David. This was some kind of cruel joke that Charles was playing. Whoever the poor child was, it would not be my son.

"Mrs. Rothenberg, we think the child here might be your David."

Detective Lauter continued to speak. Her voice seemed a million miles away. I shouted questions into the mouthpiece. Her voice echoed back into my ear. Friends pressed in to comfort me with quiet words of reassurance. I cried in disbelief. Tickets were reserved on American Airlines Flight 195 from La Guardia to Los Angeles. My sister was called. The police department was notified to page John. My boss, Mr. Scarin, rushed a secretary to the accounting department to get me five hundred dollars in traveler's checks. Walter Oerlemans volunteered to fly with me that evening to Los Angeles in case the police could not reach John. Numbers were dialed. Phones rang. The room was filled with words—quiet, frantic, disbelieving words. Questions flowed over and around me like a flood. I could not breathe. The flight to Los Angeles left La Guardia in forty minutes.

Walter helped me to the elevator. As I passed, my friends reached out to touch me. "Good luck, Marie." "I'll pray for you, Marie." "It will be okay, Marie." More words, this time giving life and hope. My muscles responded automatically. Adrenaline flowed. Somehow we found John. Somehow I made it to the plane. Then, for five hours and fifteen minutes I was locked into that jumbo jet, trying to hold off my fears, my anger, my guilt and grief.

When I talked to the detective in California I did not think it was going to be David lying in the Burn Center bed. I suppose I tried to convince myself it was someone else's child so that I could hold onto my own sanity. I even imagined that Charles had kidnapped another boy, put him in a room, and burned him to make me believe that David was dead. If the child had died, burned so badly that no one could recognize or identify him, then Charles could have taken David away. I just did not believe that Charles could do this to his own son. He loved David far too much for that.

When John and I arrived in Los Angeles, two detectives from the Buena Park Police Department met us and escorted us to a police car. Immediately we were driven to the UCI Hospital.

The detectives led us to the intensive-care unit. We passed through a cordon of police guarding David from further harm. Charles was still out there somewhere. The police feared he might return to finish what he had begun.

We entered a long, white hallway. Men and women rushed past in surgical gowns and masks. No one was speaking much. An orderly took us to a closet and handed us gowns, gloves, and masks. We helped each other tie the strings that held the mask and gown in place. We pulled on the skintight rubber gloves and placed paper shower hats over our heads.

"The boy inside has been burned quite seriously," a resident informed us. "He is covered with white ointment and a protective netting. His face and body are badly swollen. It will take some doing to recognize him even if he is your son."

Then we entered the room. "That is not David," I whispered to the resident, relieved beyond the telling; picturing David beautiful and well and smiling up at me.

"Marie, it is David," John said quietly. "Look closer."

The boy's head was huge. I could not believe that this was my son. Could that dying child be David? I looked closely at his mouth and at his shoulders. There was no longer any way to protect myself with even the smallest doubt. That burned child lying there was my son.

"David, can you hear Mommy?" I asked, leaning down and speaking into the side of that great swollen, oozing face.

Slowly, David nodded his head up and down.

I swallowed back the nausea and gripped John's arm with all the strength I could muster.

"Mommy and John are here now, Davie. Are you in pain?"

David shook his head very slowly again, this time back and forth. He was not feeling pain.

Again I spoke. "We are here, Davie, and we won't leave you. You'll be fine. You'll be okay. Rest now." A third time David nodded.

Gently the resident and John led me from the room. Outside in the hall I could not hold back my tears. As the gown was pulled off me, I began to cry. My sobs echoed up and down that hallway. John held me and still I cried. The tears came in a rush. He led me to a waiting room nearby and waited while I cried. Again hands reached out to comfort and reassure. But where was hope now?

I had assured David that he would be all right. But it took only one look to know how close to death he really was. I had promised him he would be fine. But I was not sure he would—or even should—survive in that condition, carrying such physical and emotional scars for the rest of his life. There were questions without answers. There was grief that could not be comforted. There was evil done that could not be forgiven.

I insisted on staying in the hospital through the night, but the doctors informed me there was nothing more I could do. They would spend the night trying to save him. We walked across the hall from Davie's room into another hospital room that had been transformed into a police control center. I met Detective Lauter and other members of the Buena Park Police Department.

"Where is Charles?" I asked. "Have you found him?"

"No, Mrs. Rothenberg," Sergeant Dick Hafdahl replied. "He is missing and we need your help to find him."

I began to cry again.

"You mean he could be here, in the hospital right now, waiting to try to kill David one more time?"

"We have police stationed at every important access point," the sergeant answered. His voice was gentle, caring. "We have rooms registered under false names for you and John at a nearby hotel. They, too, are guarded. We will not let Charles harm you or your family further. But we need your help in finding him."

Already they had found the hardware store where Charles had purchased the kerosene and identified the man who purchased it as my ex-husband. Already, they had bills from three different hotels Charles had stayed in that last day. Already they had traced the white Chevrolet that Charles had rented.

"We are convinced that your husband is not in this area," Sergeant Hafdahl continued.

"Where is he, then?" John interrupted.

"In San Francisco, we believe."

An attendant at the car-rental office had taken Charles to the John Wayne Airport in Orange County. The attendant watched Charles carry two suitcases into the AirCal ticket line after asking which airlines flew to San Francisco. Airline ticketing personnel remembered the standby ticket they had sold a Mr. Love for a flight to San Francisco.

"He's in San Francisco, Mrs. Rothenberg, but we need some idea from you as to where he might be or how we might find him."

Again, words filled the room. The police asked questions about Charles' past employment, about his American Express card and traveler's checks, about airline receipts and Charles' old haunts in San Francisco. Again I mumbled answers, trying to help, thinking only of my son fighting for his life in that room just a few steps away.

One last time we were gowned. One last time we watched nurses and doctors fighting to keep David alive. One last time I whispered to him, "We're here, Davie. Everything will be okay." And one more time David turned his head in my direction and nodded.

His eyes were completely swollen shut. We did not know how long he would be blind or if he would ever see again. The burned and swollen throat and the tube carrying air into his lungs prevented speech. Serious burn victims often end up mute. We did not know if he would speak again. I could feel his fear and his courage as he lay there blind and mute and helpless, listening to the voices in the room. He tried so hard to follow instructions. Somehow he knew that his life depended on it.

Then we were led back into the hallway, past the policemen guarding David's room and through the hospital lobby. The detectives escorted us to their car and drove us to our rooms at the Holiday Inn.

I do not remember sleeping that first night, but I remember the dawn. New York may have been deep in snow and slush, but that first California sunrise lit up a world all green and golden. The rain had stopped. The city had been washed clean of smog. White cumulus clouds billowed against a blue sky. Palm trees stood like silent sentinels around the Holiday Inn. Flowers bloomed in profusion. There were no screeching brakes, no sirens, no angry curses as commuters rushed to catch the subway. I stood at the window as the sun rose, and I prayed.

Prayer was not a common practice in my life. Mass in the Catholic churches I had occasionally attended as a child made God seem distant to me, like the priest, up there somewhere talking privately to God while I watched and wondered what this had to do with me. I did not pray dignified prayer-book prayers that day. I prayed foxhole prayers.

"God, let my David live!" I demanded.

And then just as strongly I would pray, "Please, God, let Davie die without more suffering."

As I stumbled through my prayers, I pictured him lying in that intensive-care center wrapped like a mummy, white and fat with swelling, unable to speak or see. And my prayers went back and forth. I would begin a prayer only to trail off as other thoughts interrupted my praying. I would ask for one thing and then demand another. Then, in the middle of a prayer I have since forgotten, the reality of the moment struck and I began to cry again.

Early that same morning, as the sun was rising, the policemen who had volunteered to guard us through the night escorted us back to the UCI Burn Center, back to David.

Dr. Robert Miller, the chief resident at UCI, invited us into a private recovery room and began to explain what lay ahead for David in the next few critical hours.

"Mrs. Rothenberg, we are doing our best to save your son's life," Dr. Miller began gently, "but at this stage there are no guarantees."

He paused for a moment, watching me intently, measuring his words.

"David has third-degree burns over approximately ninety percent of his body."

Again he paused, wondering if I understood how fragile David's hold on life really was.

"Explain what you mean by a third-degree burn," I said. "I've never really been sure what that means."

"A third-degree burn is as serious a burn as one can receive," Dr. Miller continued. "If David had been burned only to the second degree, it would mean the fire burned only partway through his skin. That would mean enough of the bottom skin layers were left that his skin could heal itself. Skin has amazing ability to fight back, to renew and replace itself. But a third-degree burn means that David's skin is destroyed all the way through to the fat layers below the skin. Ninety percent of David's skin was completely burned away. The hair follicles are gone. Every bit of skin tissue is destroyed. There is no way for the skin to replace itself. So, it will not heal on its own. It can't."

I could hear Dr. Miller clearly, but even as he spoke I pictured Davie in that fire, his skin being eaten away by the flames. I could not stop the pictures from flashing. I strained to focus on Dr. Miller. I blinked back the image of that blazing hotel room and my son inside it. But it would not go away. As he spoke, I began to tremble. John reached over to hold me. For a moment, Dr. Miller looked at me helplessly, then slowly, apologetically, he stood up and left the room. I felt John's arms around me.

"How could he do this to his own son?" I gasped. "Oh, God, how could he do it?" For a moment I tried to push John away. Like the flames that consumed my son, anger consumed me. Then I gave way to John's tight hold on me, leaned against his chest, and began to weep.

The head nurse, Sue Martinez, entered almost immediately after Dr. Miller left.

"It has been a long night, Mrs. Rothenberg, but David is doing better than we ever dreamed."

"Really?" I asked.

"Yes, really," she answered, looking me straight in the eye. "It isn't over yet. He is very critical. But is he doing better than any of us expected. We were so glad when you called," she added. "Your son was wide awake. We injected him with morphine for his pain, but he did not sleep. I called him 'honey' and 'sugar' and 'sweetheart' but I wanted so badly to call him by his name. Then you phoned.

"The police were monitoring our phone. When you telephoned from New York and asked if your son, David, was in the Burn Center, Sergeant Lauter scribbled the name on a card and handed it to me. I ran across the room and gave the card to Geri Chambers, who was monitoring David at the time.

" 'See if his name is David,' I whispered.

"She leaned down and asked your son, 'Is your name David?'

"And when he nodded," she remembered, "we almost cheered. He was not 'John Doe, child,' anymore. He was a person. He had a real name. And just hearing his own name seemed to brighten up his spirits. It sure brightened ours.

"The word spread up and down the floor," she continued. " 'His name is David.' We had a name. But David needed a person who knew more than just his name. We were so relieved to learn that you were coming on the next flight. You see, Mrs. Rothenberg, a burn patient, in fact any sick patient, can just give up and die, especially if there is no one there who loves him to call out his name. We have seen people with burns much less serious than David's just refuse to live. In fact, they will themselves to die and we can do almost nothing to save them. Then again, we have seen persons like David whose will to live is strong. He works so hard to cooperate with us even when he is in terrible pain. Now your presence here can make such a difference."

So, David works hard to cooperate, does he? I smiled to myself. *His will is strong, is it? She doesn't know the half of it. That kid's will is so strong that I thought it would kill us both.*

I remembered taking David to dinner one Sunday night four years before. Charles had been sentenced to prison the second time since our marriage for buying money orders with forged checks. I had begun divorce proceedings. And I was taking David out to dinner alone for the first time. He was two.

Davie had a little riding car he straddled and navigated around our apartment. He wanted to bring it into the restaurant and ride it. The boy was spoiled. Charles had always given David permission to do exactly what he wanted. But Charles was in prison. Raising David was my responsibility now. And I refused to let him take the toy car into the restaurant.

"David, you must leave that toy in the car. A restaurant is no place for your wheelie."

David kicked and screamed. It had always worked before.

"No, Davie," I tried to reason. "You cannot take your car inside."

He thrashed angrily, one hand in mine, the other holding onto his precious wheelie with all his might.

"No, Davie," I whispered loudly. "A restaurant is not a place to play."

Still he screamed. I felt more and more embarrassed by the commotion he was making. People were staring. I wanted to give in. Instead I picked up the toy he loved, took him firmly by the hand, walked over to a nearby garbage can, and dumped his wheelie into it.

He screamed so loudly that everybody in Brooklyn thought I must be torturing him. I marched him away from the restaurant back to the car and drove him quickly back to our apartment. He screamed the entire way. It was awful. I unlocked the door, climbed the two flights of stairs, unlocked our apartment, and we went inside.

Finally, out of breath, his screaming slowed slightly. I spoke firmly.

"Davie, if you ever do that again with another toy, I will throw that toy out, too."

He put his hands on his hips and stared up at me angrily; then he marched into his room.

I threw out a lot of toys that year—new ones, toys he really liked. I hated wasting the money Charles had spent on all those toys, but I could not give in to Davie's tantrums. I had to help him understand. He could not always have his way.

Somewhere down the road, I knew that it would make a difference.

John and I capped and gowned and masked ourselves and followed Sue Martinez into David's room. He had just come from the whirlpool. His body was completely naked. No white silvadene cream disguised the extent of his injuries. We could see blood pulsing through veins. We could see muscles contracting and expanding. We could see bone and skull. He lay there with his precious layers of skin all burned away. We could see his body working madly to keep the boy alive.

"Move your arm a little, Davie," Geri Chambers asked. And slowly, painfully, the child raised his burned and twisted arm.

"Good job, Davie," Sue Martinez praised him as she approached his bed. "Now turn on your side a little. It is time for more good stuff." Once again, he struggled to obey as Sue checked the intravenous catheters carrying life-giving nutrients into his body. Once again the nurse praised him.

Dr. Achauer entered the room and stood beside my son. "Good morning, David. Can you bend your leg?" David nodded and slowly bent his leg. From the back of the room I watched him. His head was swollen to twice its size. Ninety percent of his skin was burned away. He was in awful pain, but he was working hard to cooperate.

At that moment I was so very glad that I had had the nerve to throw his toys away. I was glad his will was strong. But I was even more glad that I had not given in to it.

"Hi, Davie," I whispered. "Mommy is very proud of you. You are a very brave boy."

I could not say more. Davie turned slowly in my direction. He could not speak or see, but he strained to feel my presence. Then he turned back toward the crowd of doctors and nurses who were working hard to save his life.

4

During David's first forty-eight hours in the hospital, almost everyone was sure my son would die. Nevertheless, doctors and nurses worked around the clock to save him.

"He is amazing," Dr. Achauer, David's surgeon, whispered to me as David was prepared for his second trip through the Burn Center to the bath. Nurses and orderlies wearing sterile gowns, masks, gloves, plastic booties, and hair covers slid David onto a gurney. One nurse temporarily disconnected from the ventilator the tubes protruding from David's throat. Another nurse protected the intravenous needles carrying fluid and nutrients into his body. Orderlies and nurses rushed David through the halls to the "hydro room." There, immediately a ventilator was attached to help David breathe. David was placed on two rubberized plastic sheets with metal frame and ropes. Then he was placed on two sliding hydraulic lifts and slowly lowered into the kidney-shaped, room-sized bath containing Betadine solution, antiseptic, and Clorox bleach. He lay completely covered by the water except for his swollen head. That area was bathed by hand.

"All we are trying to do with this solution," Dr. Achauer explained, "is to cut down the threat of infections. If we do not kill the germs attacking Davie, they will certainly kill him."

Then they rushed my son back to his room, rehooked the ventilator to the tubes stuck deep in Davie's lungs, and continued their fight to keep him alive.

Everything that could go wrong went wrong during those first few days in intensive care. Almost immediately David developed a dangerous systemic infection. His body went into stress syndrome. His kidneys, liver, and intestines tried to shut down. Doctors could not graft skin to replace skin that had been burned away until they got his system stabilized, but if they did not begin grafting almost immediately, the work to stabilize him would be useless. David would die.

Davie drifted in and out of consciousness. Nurses tried to dull his pain with morphine and then Demerol. They poured fluids into his body to replace the fluids lost in the fire. Then, those new fluids caused the body to balloon. The doctors cut slits in the burned surfaces so that the body could swell. Any moment doctors feared that David's kidneys would stop functioning entirely or that his whole system would go into terminal shock.

I stood at the end of his bed as this whirlwind of doctors and nurses blew in and out of the room. They were brilliant and committed and hardworking, but they did not know the child in that bed. To doctors and nurses alike he was "the ninety percent third-degree child in room 3B." He was a set of numbers registered on arterial lines and heart monitors. He was clinical readings. He was cc's of urine. He was pulse and blood pressure; fluids in and fluids out. He was a victim number, a patient chart, the burn boy.

I felt desperate for them to know him as I knew him. If they could only see him smile, but his face was burned away. If they could see the nose he wrinkled up at spinach and brussels sprouts, but Davie's nose was gone. If they could see his dark brown eyes, but they were swollen closed and no one knew if he would ever open them again. If they could feel his kiss on their cheeks, but even his lips had been burned off by the fire. His thick brown hair was gone. His tiny fingers and toes were charred black and ugly. He lay there burned and barely alive. He could not speak. He could not see. He was swollen to an inhuman state, but inside all that he was Davie still.

I stared at the dying child lying in the Burn Center. I closed my eyes and pictured my son lying there. At times, it was even hard for me, his mother, to remember that just beneath that awful surface, David was still a six-year-old boy. He heard what we said, even when we whispered; he felt frightened by our words or by our silence; he wanted desperately to understand what had happened and what was happening, he needed to be touched, to be held, and to be loved. I wondered what he would say if he could speak. I tried to imagine what he was feeling. I worked day and night to represent my son and his needs to the people who were treating him. I yelled for him. I cried for him. During those first days, I was my son.

"Excuse me, Marie." Dr. Achauer entered the room and approached David's bed with two new doctors in tow. He introduced me to the lung specialists from Children's Hospital and then led me to the Burn Center waiting room nearby.

"They will be performing a bronchoscopy on David," he explained. "They will place a tube down his bronchial tubes. Those are the air passageways between the mouth and the lungs. With their lighted scope the doctors will see how badly David's lungs and bronchial tubes have been damaged."

I sat on the low cushioned chair as Dr. Achauer continued his explanation.

"Those burning chemicals in the motel room produced various poison gases." Dr. Achauer spoke slowly, trying to help me grasp this new crisis in the growing list of crises David faced. "While David was in the burning room, he breathed great quantities of carbon monoxide, cyanide, and other toxic fumes produced by the fire burning the carpet and wallpaper and other synthetic materials."

"How did he live through it?" I asked.

"You've raised yourself a tough kid, Marie," Dr. Achauer answered.

"But will he make it?" I asked, feeling the tears begin to well up again.

Already I knew how Dr. Achauer hated it when I cried. Somehow I blinked back the tears that time and asked again, "Will he live?"

"We don't know. The doctors from Children's Hospital will have important information when they have finished scoping Davie. If his lungs are damaged as badly as we suspect, it won't be easy to save him."

We had not talked long when the pager on Dr. Achauer's belt signaled him to return to the Burn Center. We walked together through the halls without speaking. The two doctors waited just outside Davie's room.

I watched them whispering their prognosis in the hallway. It was immediately apparent that the news was bad. There was soot and singe in

David's bronchial tubes. The lining of his lungs was burned away. Nurses hurried in and out of David's room. I walked back to a waiting area nearby where my sister, Sandra, her husband, and John were waiting. I was still in a state of shock myself. At that moment Charles had not been arrested or imprisoned. Police guards were everywhere. Television crews, newspaper and national magazine reporters called hourly requesting interviews. Our tragedy was front-page news and the hospital corridors were lined with people watching and waiting for news of the little boy whose daddy tried to burn him to death.

"I don't think he is going to make it," I muttered as I slumped down beside John. "I don't think he *should* make it," I added angrily. "What kind of future can he have burned like that? Maybe he should die."

As we sat discussing David's terrible plight, a police guard opened the waiting-room door and interrupted.

"Marie, there is a couple here who want to see you. The man has been burned and wants to talk to you."

I panicked.

"No, I don't want to see anybody," I cried, "especially anybody who is burned. Get them out of here."

I was afraid to see someone who had been burned. I did not want to know what David would look like if he lived. I did not want to know what was waiting for us down that awful road somewhere.

"No," I said again. "I can't handle it. Later, maybe, not now. Please send them away."

"Listen, Marie," my sister cut in. "You need somebody to talk to about Davie who understands what you both are going through."

I jumped up and walked toward Sandra. "You have a lot of nerve!" I yelled at her. "What do you know? You're not going through this. I am. Davie isn't your kid. He's mine. I can only handle so much!" I said. "And I've had it. Don't do this to me."

I raged about the room a bit, while everybody waited for me to cool down. Then I sat beside John and looked to him for some support.

"I think it's a good idea, Marie," he said cautiously.

I only had enough energy left to groan in response.

"Eventually, we have to go back to New York and our jobs and families," he added. "You'll be here alone. You need somebody."

I did not speak. I could not speak. I needed somebody, all right. But whom? When hospital personnel saw my name was Rothenberg, they asked a local rabbi to visit the hospital. He came by. He was courteous.

"But I'm a Catholic," I told him. "What would I do with a rabbi?"

He laughed at the misunderstanding, offered to help me if I needed it, and then disappeared.

A Catholic priest was called to offer David last rites. When he finally arrived he stood at the door looking at my charred child and was afraid to enter. He blessed David from the doorway with a hurried sign of the cross and then he, too, disappeared.

Who would drop into our lives next? And how long before that person, too, would disappear?

I looked up at the guard, who was still waiting for instructions.

"Okay. I'll see them," I said. "But you guys stay here. Don't leave me alone with them."

There should have been music playing when Ken and Judy Curtis walked through the door that day. I should have jumped up to welcome them. These two people and their friends had come to stay. They would not disappear like the others. They would bring David and me new life by their presence. But I would discover all that later.

"Hi, Marie," Judy said, approaching me as though she were an old friend. "I'm Judy Curtis and this is my husband, Ken."

Ken had been burned in a serious industrial fire. He was spreading a highly flammable finish on a bowling-alley floor when the chemicals roared into flames around him. He ran, burning, toward nearby people. A woman tackled him and rolled out the flames, but Ken had already suffered third-degree burns over much of his body. I did not want to look up at him. I was afraid to see his face. I did not want to know what my David would look like.

"Hello, Marie," Ken said. Finally, I looked up at him. He was smiling.

"You haven't been burned," I said, surprised at how good he looked. "I just don't believe you have been burned."

We all sat amazed as Ken, still grinning, peeled away a skintight glove and rolled up one pant leg. He did not say much. He just showed me the scars running up and down his hands and legs. They were not ugly scars. They were flat and firm, the color of baby skin. He took my hand and guided it over a long scar on his side. There was a look of caring in his eyes but he did not say much. "We would like to have a prayer with you, Marie. Would that be all right?"

I do not remember having experienced prayer just like that before. Judy reached out and took my hand. Ken took John's hand in his. My sister and brother-in-law were just as surprised and taken off guard as we were as they joined in the circle. Judy and Ken bowed their heads and closed their eyes while the four of us looked back and forth at each other, not knowing exactly how to respond. Then Judy began to talk to God the way people talk to each other.

In my experience you talked to saints or to Mary but you did not talk directly to God. Besides, I had been angry at God for a long time. My prayers had not been answered. Where was God when Charles picked up David and took him to California? Where was God when Charles struck the match and drove away as the room exploded into flame? Where was God now as David lay dying in the room across the hall?

"We need You to help us, Lord," Judy began her prayer. "Little Davie is burned very badly. He needs You to heal him. Please, Lord, heal him as You promised. And be with Marie and her friends and family. Give them strength to face whatever Your will is for Davie's life. Help them handle this thing. Thank You for Your Son, Jesus. Amen."

When Judy finished her prayer, I was trembling. I felt every word she said through my entire body. I got such a weird feeling inside of me as she prayed. Judy hugged me. Ken hugged me. They shook hands with John and my family. Then they were gone. Somehow, I knew they would be back. They would not leave me.

I started to cry. "There is hope," I said. "If this man almost died from his burns, then there is hope for David."

John came over to me and took me in his arms.

"People do get better, John," I said to him. "Maybe Davie can get better, too."

For those first two or three days at the UCI Burn Center, I was, in my son's words, a basket case. My police guard led me from hospital to hotel in a kind of trance. I seemed to always be crying or fainting or throwing up. I stared uncomprehendingly at old magazines in the intensive-care waiting room. Nothing seemed in focus. John, my sister and her husband, doctors and nurses, and police talked to me but I found it difficult to concentrate on what they were saying. I think my system, like David's, was in some kind of shock, only nobody knew how to treat the kind of shock I felt until Ken and Judy entered our lives.

Understand, I am not a naturally religious person. I do not find it easy to talk about God. I do not find it appropriate to grab hands with strangers and pray. "Praise the Lord" or "God bless you" are expressions that do not come automatically from my lips. I am from Brooklyn, after all, and you have to be tough to survive in Brooklyn. If my childhood in Pennsylvania and New York taught me anything, it was that you used more than prayers and Bible verses to survive.

When I was six years old, David's age, I lived in an old house in Scranton, Pennsylvania, with my mother. One winter day my mother told me to get coal from the basement and stock the fire. I did not have any slippers on. I tried to explain that my brother, Allen, had my slippers in his room.

"Stay away from Allen," she warned me. "Get the coal now!" (I was afraid to go into that freezing basement coal bin without my slippers.)

Allen was retarded and my mother kept him locked in a room upstairs. When she was not looking, I sneaked into Allen's room to get my slippers and my mother caught me there.

"Get out of this room!" she screamed at me, and when I could not move fast enough to please her, she threw me against an old couch with an iron rail. In the beating that followed she dislocated my hip. I could not walk without crying from the pain.

My mother was an alcoholic. She was drunk most of the time. When she saw the damage her abuse had caused me, she was afraid. My hip and leg were twisted and swollen. The pain was awful. Still, my mother could not risk taking me to the hospital for treatment. So she kept me home. When I could not make it to the bathroom, she just picked me up under one arm and carried me there. The pain and swelling grew worse. When the principal called to inquire about my absence, my mother lied. Finally, my father heard rumors about the "accident," came to my mother's house, and simply took me from her.

For a while I lived with my father and my aunt. Already she was responsible to care for my two older sisters. I was one more mouth to feed. She called me "Little Devil." She teased and tormented me. When my father remarried, I was sent back to live with my mother again. She still hated me. I was eight or nine years old. One morning, drunk and crazy, my mother chased me with a beer bottle, screaming that she would kill me. I slid under an old bed with rusty iron springs. I hooked my fingers into those rigid springs and pulled myself up so that when my mother tried to poke me out with a broom handle she would miss me. I hung on as she poked and probed and swung the broom beneath the bed. Finally, she left the room.

I was afraid my mom would hurt me. When I heard her snoring, I quickly crawled out from under the bed. Afraid I would make trouble for her with my dad again, she had hidden my jacket and my winter shoes. It was snowing but I had to find him. My mother had fallen into a drunken stupor across the doorway to prevent my escape. In the darkness I found my sneakers and put them on. I had no socks and went outside into the blizzard wearing a sweater and an old pair of pants. We lived in Scranton, quite a walk from my father's house, in an area that was very isolated. There was a phone booth near a service station on a nearby corner. I could barely reach the phone and I had no idea how to get the operator without money. Somehow an operator came on the line.

"I want my dad," I cried into the telephone.

"Do you know his number?" the operator asked.

"No, please get me my daddy."

I must have been crying very loudly. A man in a nearby apartment heard me and came out to the phone booth. I was terrified. I pushed against the door to keep him out, still trying to get the operator to find my father. I was pushing against the door and screaming. A police car stopped. The man explained. They took me from the booth and placed me up against the squad car heater. I was practically frostbitten. The neighbor knew my father and told the police officer where he lived. When they walked me up the stairs to my dad's house, my new stepmother took me in and bathed me and gave me a place to stay.

Almost immediately there were problems. She had her own children. My sisters already put an added drain on their household bills. She and my father fought. We were quarantined to our rooms. We could not even eat at the same table with my stepmother and her family. One day when my father brought a plate of food to my room, my stepmother had a fit of anger.

"It's her or me!" she screamed at my father. Then she began to throw my father's clothes down the steps and out of the house. I got scared.

"Clarissa," I said to my sister, "I can't let this happen. I'm leaving. I'm going to go right now. I'm just going to take my schoolbooks and I'm moving out."

I ran away to a girl friend's home and lived with her family for a whole year. I was in the seventh grade. After a year my father met me in the street outside the school and said, "If you don't come home by tomorrow, you're going to an orphanage to live permanently." I didn't have a choice. I moved back home and the day I did, my stepmother came into my sister's room and started beating me. She hit me so hard I thought she had broken my eardrum. My sister grabbed her and began to scream.

"You're a witch!" she said. "You threw her out and now that our dad orders her back, you beat her. You have no right to hit Marie!"

Later that evening, my father entered my room and began shouting.

"If you cause me any more humiliation," he yelled at me, "I will kill you." Then he threw me up against the radiator and began to kick me.

I was grounded. When I came home from school I had to do my chores and go straight to my room. I could not go out anywhere or do anything with my classmates. I quit school in my teens and went to work in a factory in Scranton bagging dresses after they were pressed. I was a good bagger. I liked making a living. I missed school, but having an income gave me some independence.

Soon after I quit school, my father was taken to the VA hospital with terminal cancer. I'd left home and moved in with friends again.

On his deathbed my dad asked that I make peace with my stepmother. He wanted me to promise that I would move back home to help her raise his sons. My father looked so thin and frightened. He held my shoulder in his bony hand and insisted that I promise to take care of his wife and her family. I could not lie to him on his deathbed. I refused. A day and a half later, he died. I moved to New York to live with my sisters. I returned to high school and nine months later received my diploma and entered Bernard Baruch College. I have been on my own ever since.

I always felt that if I could handle my childhood, I could handle anything. Then I met and married Charles and plunged into a seven-year nightmare that ended with his attempted murder of my son. I thought I could survive any crisis if I were tough enough. But looking down on my dying child in the UCI Burn Center, knowing that my ex-husband had done this to him, wondering where Charles was and what he would do to us next, left me with a crisis I was not tough enough to handle. At the heart of it all were my mixed feelings about David. At least part of the time I was praying that Davie would die. I loved my child. I wanted him to have the chance to grow up like a normal boy, but watching him struggle for life in the Burn Center left me feeling hopeless. When I saw him suffering I wanted God to take him, to end it. I begged the nurses to explain why they were keeping him hanging on this way.

"Why don't you just let him go?" I cried. "Why should he suffer more?"

A priest from a nearby parish scolded me for praying that God would take my child home.

"You cannot tell God to take David," he warned me. "You have to ask God to do what He thinks is best. Then you will be able to accept what has happened to him."

That advice made me angry. I could never accept what Charles had done to Davie. I could not sit back and let doctors and nurses keep my son alive if he would not lead at least some kind of normal life when they discharged him back into my keeping. Of course I felt terrible grief just thinking about Davie's death, but I felt even worse thinking how it might be if he lived.

So I prayed that God would take David to heaven to be with Him. I had never thought anything about life after death. I did not know what I believed about heaven or even if I was sure there *was* a heaven. But I knew there must be someplace where little children did not have to suffer. I thought it cruel of God to leave David on the earth in such misery. "God's will be done," the priest had said.

Hasn't Davie been through enough? I answered to myself angrily.

As I watched what was left of my child fighting for life, I felt terribly guilty for wanting him to die. *How could I really love him,* I asked myself, *if I want my own son to die?* My feelings went back and forth. "Is he better off living or better off dead?" I was making myself sick from worrying. I did not understand what to do. I did not know how to pray. I did not know what I should ask God to do. There were doctors and nurses, pain pills and tranquilizers, burn centers and intensive-care units to take care of the body. But my crisis was in the heart, and there was no one there who could help me through it.

"Good morning, Marie." Judy stuck her head inside the waiting room the very next morning after we first met. Ken stood nearby.

"You're back," I said, wondering why it felt so good to see them. They were not like me. They smiled too much. Our backgrounds were entirely different. Their personalities and life-styles and mine were miles apart. But I felt good when they walked into the room.

"We brought a Bible, Marie," Judy said, sitting down in the waiting room, "just in case you need it."

They placed the Bible on the chair beside me. I do not remember ever having read the Bible. I did not have the first idea about using it. But it seemed important to them that I take it, so I did.

"You really believe that God could do something for Davie, don't you?" I said to Ken. He nodded and smiled but said nothing. "How can you be so sure He actually hears your prayers?" I asked.

"Oh, that's easy," Judy laughed. "Want an example? We've prayed and God has answered our prayers in the last twenty-four hours."

"Come on," I answered skeptically.

"Really!" Judy said leaning forward with a smile. "Want to hear a good story?"

What could I say? I knew Judy was going to tell her story anyway. Besides, I wanted proof that God could hear and answer prayers more than I wanted anything in the world.

"Yesterday," Judy began, "we were driving home from a wedding. We heard another story on the car radio about you and Davie and the Burn Center. We just had the strongest, strongest feeling that God wanted us to come down here to see you and find out if we could lend you a helping hand. So we turned around and drove directly to the UCI Burn Center.

"When we got here and saw how many buildings there were, we didn't have the slightest idea where you would be. So we spent a couple of minutes in the parking lot asking God to direct us."

Ken and Judy sat on either side of me, both leaning toward me now. Judy had her hand on my knee. Ken smiled and nodded. They were unreal. And what they were saying to this tough kid from Brooklyn seemed straight from some other world.

"After we prayed," Judy continued, "we began to walk among the maze of buildings. We practically ran into a young woman coming out of a hospital back entrance. She was wearing a name tag. So we stopped her and asked if she could direct us to the Burn Center.

" 'Yes,' she said, 'go through the door I just came out and you'll be there!' "

Judy giggled. "So we came into the Burn Center through the back door, got on an elevator, walked up to a policeman guarding an empty hall, and asked him where the intensive-care unit was.

" 'You're standing in front of it,' he answered. 'Just go right in.' "

If Ken and Judy had walked into the front entrance of the Burn Center, they would not have gotten past hospital security or the police guard there. Hundreds of people milled about the Burn Center lobby. The press and the public had been barred from our area. Davie was struggling to live. The hospital gave regular reports on his progress, but no one was allowed inside. The hospital refused to jeopardize David's fragile health for any reason.

"A nurse came up to us and asked us why we were in the Burn Center," Judy was saying.

"We want to see Marie Rothenberg," Ken had explained to her. "I am a burn victim myself and I think I can help her."

I wondered that day why the nurse had not called security to have Ken and Judy thrown out.

Ken picked up the story. "The nurse took us to a policeman on guard outside your room. He poked his head inside and you said you would talk to us. You see, Marie," he continued, "we prayed in the parking lot and by the time we got to your floor on the Burn Center, our prayers were answered."

For a moment I stared at them. I did not know whether to call the guard and get these loonies off my hands or to throw my arms around them. For a moment I stared at Ken and Judy in disbelief. I, too, had prayed, in my own stumbling way that morning at the Holiday Inn, that somehow God would send me somebody to help me know how to pray for Davie. It seemed that God might have heard my prayers, too.

"How should I pray for Davie?" I asked, choking back the tears.

Ken and Judy both placed their hands on me. They spoke quietly. Their words gave comfort. Some I heard. Some I did not. It was not what they said, exactly, that made the difference. It was how they said it. They seemed so sure about God, that He did hear and answer prayers. And as they shared I began to believe it myself. Then, they asked to pray with me again.

"Dear Father," Judy began, "take Marie's little David. She doesn't want him to suffer anymore. He is Your child, really. You make the decision whether David should live with us or live with You. She is tired of trying to decide. You promised not to give us anything we couldn't handle. You promised not to give Davie anything he couldn't handle, now or in the future. So we leave Davie, Your child, in Your loving hands and trust You to do Your very best for him. Whatever You decide, Lord, we will love and trust You forever."

A nurse opened the door. "You and your friends can see David now," she said.

Ken and Judy walked with me to the gowning area. They suited up like old-timers. When they entered the room, Davie was lying on the bed covered with Silvadene cream. His legs had been slit wide open from his ankles to his hips to allow for the swelling. He was stapled back together with large, cardboard staples. Tubes ran down his nose and throat. Other tubes were fastened to intravenous bottles hanging above his bed. His head was twice its normal size. His eyes were still sealed closed. Nurses were dressing the bloody, open wounds with Silvadene cream. Davie was groaning and slightly rocking back and forth in pain.

For a moment I trembled with rage and worry. Then Ken put his arm around me and Judy grasped my hand.

"Davie is God's child, Marie. Let God take care of him."

For a moment I fought their advice. Then I relaxed. Again I gave David back to God, and a load of fear slipped off my shoulders. I had spent the past four days worrying about so many things that only God could handle. *Will Davie live or die? Should Davie live or die? Will he see again? Will he speak again? What will he look like? How will he support himself? Who will marry him?* Now, I placed Davie and all those worries about his future in God's hands. I would worry about helping Davie through each day, one day at a time. The rest was God's problem, not mine.

"Davie," I said, leaning down to whisper, "everything is going to be all right." As we stood there looking down on that charred little body, I felt it might be true.

5

A Buena Park policeman stood on guard just outside David's hospital room. Another police officer monitored the phone in the police center across the hallway. There was a policeman guarding John and me, and twenty-four-hour police protection at our rooms in the Holiday Inn. No one could be sure what Charles would do next.

I was afraid that he would return to threaten David again. I didn't know if he would suddenly appear in the hospital corridor or in the hall outside my room. I even wondered if he might try to shoot John or me as we traveled back and forth from the hospital to the hotel or in the cafeteria or in the nearby shopping mall where we sometimes walked to stretch our legs and share our grief. That first week, I was afraid almost all the time; afraid for Davie in his struggle to live, afraid for me, afraid for John. Without the Buena Park Police Department, I don't know how I could have survived those fears. What I didn't know then was that all the police officers guarding us were volunteering to do it on their own time. During regular working hours, besides their regular and emergency tasks, the entire Buena Park Police Department joined forces with other police and sheriff units across the nation to find and capture Charles.

On the night of our arrival in Southern California, before returning to the hospital, John and I were talking to the officers who were guarding us. We sat down in the room they occupied and I noticed the sketch of a man's face hanging from a paper clip attached to the wall.

"Who's that?" I asked the officer.

"That's Charles," he answered.

"That's not Charles!" I screamed. "That's nobody. No wonder you can't find him. You're looking for the wrong man."

I was bounding about the room in a complete state of shock. All this protection was guarding us from the wrong man. I hadn't thought to bring a photo. They used witnesses to describe Charles and a police artist had assembled the composite sketch. It wasn't close to resembling Charles.

John and the policeman moved to calm me. "Your sister Sandra has already been called to find recent pictures of Charles," the officer informed us. "She is on her way here to deliver them."

I have two sisters. Sandra lives with her family in Brooklyn. Clarissa and her family live in Jersey City, New Jersey.

The New York Police Department had a black-and-white booking photo of Charles that had been taken when he was arrested for forgery in 1978. Red lights flashing and sirens blaring, the photo was rushed to my sister Sandra. Sandra took the photo to the airport and flew with it to California. Within a day the Buena Park Police Department released the real photo of my ex-husband to the various police units searching for him across the country.

Police from Buena Park put together a paper lineup which included photos of five nonsuspects and the black-and-white photo of Charles. Charles was the photo marked number 3. Police showed the lineup to all the motel clerks. The Holiday Inn desk clerk immediately identified Charles and remembered talking to him on his arrival and departure from the motel.

"It had been raining for days," she remembered. "Mr. Rothenberg asked me several times where he could take his son to entertain him since Disneyland and the other parks were closed. He also talked about his ex-wife having a boyfriend who was a cop. He said they were from New York. He called it a 'vicious place.' He thought he and his wife would probably still be married if they had stayed in California."

The clerk was off work several days following that conversation. On the day Charles tried to murder David she saw my ex-husband again as he was hurriedly checking out and heading for the airport.

"When he checked out of our motel," she informed the police, "I asked him about his son. He said something about his son having a terminal illness and that he didn't have long to live."

Charles, for reasons known only to himself, had also checked into a third room in the Quality Inn motel nearby. Buena Park police staked out the room still registered to Charles, hoping he might return. When Charles didn't appear, they obtained a search warrant. Inside the room, they found David's clothing, his schoolbooks, homework, and his toys. There was a large new suitcase there as well, filled with clothing left by Charles.

We had obtained several photos of Charles by then. One, a picture taken at Christmas, seemed especially ironic. Charles and David were sitting next to Santa Claus. They were both smiling. In all the pictures I have of them together, it is obvious how much Charles seemed to love our son.

All the people interviewed by the Buena Park police investigating team reported the same reactions. Charles and David seemed to be a perfect father-son combination. They remembered Charles as a doting father. And David seemed a normal, happy son. The attendants at the handball court remembered how much fun father and son had playing video games in the lobby. Even Buena Park policemen who played handball there regularly remembered seeing David and Charles playing those games together.

After he tried to murder David, Charles seemed obsessed by his son's condition. During those days when Charles was at large, he called the UCI Burn Center and the Buena Park police time and time again for information about his son. Sometimes he pretended to be a concerned citizen. Other times he claimed to be a paramedic or a fireman still interested in the case. But at least six times he called the police station, admitted who he was, and carried on long conversations with Sergeant Dick Hafdahl, the investigating officer on David's case, and other policemen on duty. Those conversations were recorded. They are a strange testament to a father's twisted concern for the son he tried to murder.

In the first call, Charles identified himself to Lieutenant Gary Rooney.

"Are you connected with the boy who was burned?" Charles asked the policeman.

"That's right," Rooney answered.

"Okay," Charles replied, "I'm his father."

"You're his father?" Rooney said, surprised the suspect would call the police station and identify himself so plainly.

"Right," answered Charles. "How is David?"

"I don't know," Rooney claimed. "I haven't been over there [UCI Burn Center]. I'll try to get Sergeant Hafdahl for you. He's the one handling the case. Can you hold on?"

"Well, only for about thirty seconds," Charles replied.

Then as the dispatcher attempted to transfer the call to Sergeant Hafdahl, Charles asked three times in a row, "How's my son? How's my son? How's my son?"

Charles called back nineteen minutes later. He seemed desperate to know if David had survived.

"How's David?" Charles asked.

"Well, he's alive," Sergeant Hafdahl answered.

"I wanna know . . . what's . . . what's . . ." Charles searched for words.

"I'm telling you the truth," Hafdahl cut in. "He's alive."

"How bad is he?" Charles questioned.

"Well, he's burned," Hafdahl answered, playing for time.

"How bad?" Charles asked again.

"Well, I don't know yet," Hafdahl answered.

"Was everything burned?" Charles asked.

"You mean the room?" Hafdahl stalled.

"No, I'm talking about his body," Charles cut in angrily.

"No, no, no." Again Hafdahl stalled.

"Was his face burned?"

"I haven't seen him," Hafdahl answered.

Later in that call, Charles said, "I'd love to see my kid." When Hafdahl encouraged Charles to turn himself in, Charles agreed and asked, "There's just one thing I want to know—what's the chance of my son living?"

In the third call Charles asked again, "Truthfully, will my son live?" Hafdahl stalled, parceling out information, trying to keep Charles on the phone, trying to discover exactly where he was. Charles said he was willing to come to Los Angeles and turn himself in. Finally he blurted out, " 'Cause I love my son and I've ruined it now, and I know that. . . ."

But Charles did not keep his agreement to meet officers in San Francisco or in Orange County. He did not turn himself in. Instead, on Friday, March 4, Charles sent a telegram to the police in Buena Park.

". . . By the time you receive this telegram," he wrote, "I will have already landed in a foreign country with help from a close friend where . . . let's see . . . where I will permanently stay. Now I realize I will never see my son again. I also realize the reality that will happen to me if I'm ever captured. So I left and have now relieved myself of any physical harm to me and will cause no more to others."

Five days later, Charles called the police in Buena Park one last time. He said he was in Bermuda or near it. He said he was "extremely scared and very weary." Charles expressed concern about his own safety and then asked one more time, "I just want to know how my . . . if my kid was gonna make it or not."

How does one explain a man who tries to murder his son and then seems so sincerely concerned about the boy's recovery? Everybody asks me why he did it. I don't know. In those phone calls to the Buena Park police he left many clues.

In the last call, Sergeant Hafdahl directly asked Charles why he did it.

"A lot of it had to do with her [Marie], you know, her boyfriend, John the cop, you know, the way I've been basically abused and that. . . ."

He was angry at me for allowing John to be with David while he was in prison.

"I have a past criminal record," Charles said in one call to Sergeant Hafdahl. "For the last years, while I was in prison, you know, it wasn't too nice to be having . . . letting [him] have rights to my son."

Charles felt he had been mistreated by John and me while he was in prison and during the times between.

"I [have] been threatened, abused, and I didn't want her to have David anymore," Charles claimed. "I love my child. I don't know why I did what I did. I just didn't want her to have him anymore."   .

If Charles weren't so sick, I would have been enraged by his false accusations to the police in those phone calls from his place of hiding. He was angry that I had exclusive rights to David while he was in prison. He was angry that John, my fiancé, saw David so much during the years since our divorce. And with his two prison terms and his night shifts as a waiter, Charles was angry that he could afford so little time with David himself. However, quite to the contrary of Charles' angry accusations in his phone calls to the police and in his interviews with the press, John and I had done everything possible to guarantee that he had time with David. Last Christmas was just one example.

Charles was discharged from prison. He had no family. I figured he was alone. David was his son. We should share the holidays. So I suggested to John that we take Charles in for the Christmas season. John thought it strange. Now, I don't blame him.

"This is crazy, Marie," John said to me three days before Christmas

59

Eve. "I'm telling my friends that I'm going to my fiancée's house for Christmas. Her ex-husband is going to be there, too. We're all going to exchange gifts around the tree."

"Do this for Charles, John," I said, smiling sheepishly. "Would you like to be alone for the holidays? How would you feel if you had nowhere to go? Charles has no one. Let's be nice."

John agreed.

Picture it. Christmas Eve. John, my fiancé, Charles, my ex-husband, David, and our wider family eating together, singing carols together, and exchanging gifts. I even borrowed my fiancé's car to take my ex-husband shopping for David's presents.

At the end of the evening, Charles asked, "Can I come back at five o'clock in the morning to watch David open his gifts under the tree?"

Would you believe it? I said yes.

In fact, I almost never said no to this man. And on those few times I did say it, he made me feel so bad and guilty that I had to change my mind and say yes. I gave in to him because he scared me. I didn't want trouble from Charles. I was afraid he would flip out. In two years, perhaps twice I had to say no to one of Charles' requests to see David, because David and I had already made other plans. And this man told the world he tried to murder his son because I wouldn't let him see the boy.

I knew he was dangerous, but I learned too late how dangerous he was. I knew he could not be trusted, but I had no idea how well and how often he lied. Now he was on the loose and I was afraid for all of us. No one could even guess what Charles might do next.

"I don't wanna hurt Marie or anyone," Charles promised in one call to the police. "I don't plan to do it. I don't carry a gun."

When Hafdahl reminded him that he had carried a gun in New York, Charles said, "Yeah, a long time ago."

Later in that same call he said, "Just tell Marie that no one's gonna hurt anybody. I don't wanna get involved. Okay?"

Charles could not be trusted. His telephone promises sounded like threats. The police stood their ground. Twenty-four-hour security was maintained for John and me. The manhunt continued for seven long days.

The police and I were amazed at how little history Charles seemed to have. Charles claimed to be an orphan. When he was asked to list a close friend or next of kin, he always wrote the name Father Ronald Connors, now a Catholic bishop serving in the Dominican Republic. At various times Charles claimed to have been raised by Father Connors, to have met him while working in the Peace Corps in the Dominican Republic, and to have worked with Father Connors as a volunteer in his parish in Santo Domingo.

I had heard Charles' stories about Bishop Connors for seven years. Finally, Buena Park police contacted Father Connors in Santo Domingo. After everything else they had heard of Charles, the police were surprised even to find a Bishop Connors in the Dominican Republic. He told Detective David Skaugstad of the Buena Park police that he had known Charles since the early 1960s when Charles was in jail in New York City. He had been referred to Charles by a Puerto Rican family who wanted to see if Father Connors could offer the prisoner any assistance. Charles was only a teenager at the time. Apparently he formed quite an attachment to the young priest who visited him. Over the years my ex-husband made up all the stories about their long-term history. Connors did not "raise" Charles and he didn't know of any priest in New York who had. Connors was under the impression that Charles had been raised by an uncle [Saul] who supposedly lived in California. The police could find no way to verify that claim, either.

When the police told Bishop Connors about Charles' attempted murder of his son, Connors was totally surprised. Three years before, Charles had told Bishop Connors that my son and I were killed in a tragic automobile accident. Connors and the police concluded that Charles told the lies about our deaths because he was embarrassed to tell the bishop about our divorce.

Charles had not worked with Bishop Connors in Santo Domingo in the Peace Corps. He had not even visited the bishop or his parish there. Most of the stories Charles had told of their relationship had been lies.

Detective Petkiewitz from the New York Police Department called with other information that concerned us all. He had spoken to Charles' girl friend. She had reported that Charles had flown to California with a great deal of money. She said Charles claimed to have saved fifteen thousand dollars while working at Luchow's Restaurant. A new manager at Luchow's claims that Charles was fired for stealing but he didn't know how much had been stolen. The New York police had found the serial numbers of the traveler's checks Charles had purchased. He was carrying thirteen thousand dollars. That much money made it easy for Charles to stay on the run for quite a long time. There were bulletins out across the country for his arrest. His picture was in every police and sheriff station. Officers searched bus and rail terminals, airports and hotels.

As the search continued, I told the police that Charles was a person who liked familiar surroundings. If he was in San Francisco, he would probably be at the Monroe Residence Club. Two Buena Park policemen were immediately dispatched to San Francisco with a warrant for Charles' arrest. They asked the hotel's desk clerk if anyone fitting Charles' description had rented a room there in the last few days. The clerk clearly remembered renting Charles a room.

Apparently the morning after David had been burned, Charles did fly to San Francisco. At half-past four in the afternoon he had rented room 209 at the Monroe Residence Club. He paid $320.00 in traveler's checks to guarantee a month's rent. He then told the clerk that he had to pick up some things at the San Francisco YMCA. Unfortunately, when San Francisco police came to the hotel that day on a telephone tip from the Buena Park police to see if Charles had checked in there, the clerk saw my ex-husband watching the police from a telephone booth on the corner of Van Ness and Sacramento, looking in the direction of the hotel. Charles did not return to his room. For twenty-four hours police maintained surveillance on room 209. Surveillance was also maintained on the YMCA hotel on Golden Gate Avenue.

When Charles did not appear, Buena Park police flew an officer to San Francisco with a search warrant to enter room 209. The police found Charles' luggage and most of his belongings there.

Every policeman and policewoman in San Francisco was given a copy of the black-and-white photo of Charles. With the gruesome details of Charles' crime in every newspaper and on every television and radio station in the city, the search became a rather personal matter for law-enforcement officers there. Thursday, eight days after his crime, Charles was seen by a policeman just outside the YMCA on Golden Gate Avenue. Officers approached Charles and spoke softly.

"Do you know why we're here?" one officer said.

"Yes," answered Charles, "I do."

Eyewitnesses reported that Charles was calm, almost relieved to be in custody. Immediately he was transported to the San Francisco Hall of Justice. San Francisco police informed Buena Park police of Charles' arrest. Sergeant Hafdahl and a second officer flew to San Francisco to complete a search warrant for Charles' last known address and to return him to Southern California.

Sergeant Hafdahl arrived the next morning at the Hall of Justice to arrange for Charles' transport back to Orange County. Because of a paperwork blunder, there was no Rothenberg listed as a prisoner on any of the retaining floors. Hafdahl and his partner began another search to find Charles, this time floor by floor in the San Francisco Hall of Justice. On the seventh floor, Hafdahl recognized Charles standing only ten or fifteen feet away.

"Hi, Charles," Hafdahl said, approaching my ex-husband. "Do you know who I am?"

Charles had spoken to the officer on the telephone at least five times during the past days.

"Yes," Charles answered. "I recognize your voice. How's my son?"

"David is in very critical condition," Hafdahl answered. "He has second and third degree burns over ninety percent of his body, but he's still alive."

Charles asked two other questions he had asked in every telephone conversation: "Who came with Marie to Los Angeles?" and "Has this been in the papers?"

A San Francisco detective was about to lead Charles away when he asked Hafdahl if they could speak for a moment in confidence. Hafdahl later told me how they moved off into a corner of the large, congested room. Again Charles begged for more information about David. Then in a whisper he confided, "There is thirteen thousand dollars in traveler's checks in my room at the YMCA. I want the money to go to Marie."

Hafdahl and his partner went to Room 821 in the YMCA. It had been registered to David Love. They showed their search warrant to the policemen stationed at the doorway and entered the room. They removed all of Charles' personal property, including approximately twenty pictures he had tacked to the wall above his bed. They were pictures of David, of me, and of our family when we were still a family.

In the holding tank in Judge Rheinheimer's courtroom, Charles said again, this time to the deputy public defender, that he wanted the thirteen thousand dollars to go to his son. There was no evidence presented that the money had been stolen. The judge ordered a freeze on the money until the issues could be sorted out. Charles was driven in a police bus the four hundred miles from San Francisco to Orange County. The nationwide manhunt for David's father and my ex-husband had finally ended.

Later, in an interview with a police psychologist, Charles was overheard discussing his crime.

"I don't know why I did it that way," he said. "After I did my son I was going to kill myself and I became scared and could not do it."

Again he partially blamed me for his crime. He told the psychologist how I wanted to take his son away from him. "That is one of the reasons I did it," he is reported to have said. He also claimed that he did not want to leave his son all alone when he killed himself, and that was why he wanted to kill his son. "I've been thinking of doing it for a while," he added. Charles also said he didn't want to go to trial. He just wanted to plead guilty and get it over with.

When Charles was arrested, I was sick in my bed at the Holiday Inn in Buena Park. I had bronchitis and couldn't stop coughing. I had a 104-degree temperature. I was sick and miserable and afraid. David was barely clinging to life. John had to return to his job in New York. And Charles was still eluding arrest. Suddenly there was a light tap on the door.

"Come in," I called out between coughing fits.

The room filled up with police. The men and women who had been guarding us around the clock were all there. They were laughing and talking loudly about San Francisco and Charles and about getting some sleep at last.

"What are you guys doing in here?" I rasped.

"We found him," they said almost in unison. "We can go home now. You're safe."

"No," I said, jumping up in bed. "You can't go home yet, not until I see a picture of him arrested and in handcuffs. He's going to come back and get me the minute you guys leave. I know it."

I was really scared. The officers had missed Charles so many times. They had confused him with so many other people. What if this announcement was another mistake? I could not believe them or share their relief.

"No, Marie," one tried to convince me. "This time they got him. He's in custody in San Francisco. You can relax."

Somebody turned on the television news. Almost immediately I saw Charles on the screen. He was under arrest in San Francisco. An anchorman was speaking.

"A New York man accused of setting his son on fire in a Buena Park motel room appeared relieved today after officers arrested him at a local San Francisco YMCA."

The officers in my hotel room cheered. We laughed and applauded like children. The newsman continued speaking.

"At the time of his arrest, Charles David Rothenberg, forty-two, of Brooklyn, New York, was wearing a pin that said, 'Kids are special.' "

The laughter died. Officers filed from my room. And I was left to cry.

6

Charles had been arrested. One pressure had been relieved. Now we could focus entirely on David's fight for life. The news had not been good. His infections were spreading. The grafting process had been slowed. Lung specialists found the lining of David's lungs to be severely damaged by the flames and poisonous fumes. John and I sat in the intensive-care unit waiting for more bad news.

Dr. Achauer walked into the room, dressed for surgery.

"It has been quite a night," he smiled, slumping down on the sofa beside us. "The little guy is putting up quite a fight."

"What's happening to his lungs?" John asked.

"Good things," Dr. Achauer answered. "Davie's lungs seem to be clearing up themselves. There would be little chance for us to clean out lining that is that seriously damaged, but Davie's lungs have been sloughing off the sooty and singed tissue all through the night. Even the specialists are amazed that his first signs of healing are so radical and early."

"Does that mean he's going to make it?" I asked.

"We're a long way from knowing that," Dr. Achauer answered honestly. "I've quit trying to outguess Davie. I didn't dream we could keep him alive the first twenty-four hours. Then I gave him only forty-eight hours more and he fooled me again. Who knows what that little fighter in there can do. All we can do is help him in the fight."

When I was still in New York the day we learned about the fire, police officials told my office manager to prepare me for Davie's death. Dr. Miller instructed our police guards to stay with us that first night because he would probably be bringing us news of Davie's passing. After the lung specialists came, Dr. Achauer tried to prepare us for the inevitable bad news; still, Davie refused to give up.

"Let's get our gowns on," Dr. Achauer instructed. "Davie could use a visit from his mom about now."

"Is he conscious?" I asked.

"Conscious and coughing," Achauer replied.

John and I entered the room again. "Hi, David," I whispered, leaning down toward him. "Mommy and John are here."

Davie moved his swollen head in my direction. He couldn't see. He couldn't speak. He was coughing up lining from his damaged lungs. I could feel him leaning toward me, wanting to ask a hundred questions.

"Davie, I know you want to talk, honey, but right now you have to be patient and wait a while longer."

Strange guttural sounds came up through Davie's throat. What voice he had filtered through burned and bleeding tissue and around the tubes forced down his throat and into his lungs. There was no way for me to understand those tiny painful gasps he made, or what he was trying so desperately to tell me.

"I don't know how long it will be, Davie." I hoped that I was guessing the question he was trying to ask. "Be patient, and before you know it you will be talking again."

David made a few more gurgling sounds. After another bout of coughing he stopped trying to speak and just lay there, tilted slightly in my direction. How I wanted to signal my love to him, but I couldn't even see a place on his body that I could touch. He was one open, bleeding wound.

"Everything is going to be fine, Davie," I said to my son over and over again. I didn't know whether he would live or die, but I wanted to say something to encourage him in his fight for life.

"We have a surprise for you, Davie," I said, opening the box I carried. I placed a new portable tape recorder and a set of tapes with Davie's favorite songs on the shelf above his bed. John and I had purchased quite a collection of pleasant, familiar music.

John opened the batteries and attached the speakers. I placed the first tape on the machine. Immediately the intensive-care room was filled with music.

It's a world of laughter, a world of tears;
it's a world of hopes and a world of fears.
There's so much that we share
that it's time we're aware.
It's a small world after all.

When the music began, Davie's head jerked forward in the direction of the speakers.

"Can you hear it, Davie?" I said, seeing his whole body move awkwardly to the rhythms of that song. Davie loved to dance. Before his burns, he tap-danced about our apartment in Brooklyn. He especially loved the theme music from the Small World ride in Disneyland. He had the record in our apartment and had played it until it was scratchy and almost worn out.

Nurses stuck their heads into the room and smiled.

"What's all the racket?" a nurse questioned.

I prepared myself to do battle to save Davie's music. I had cleared the recorder with a doctor but doctors breeze in and out on their rounds. It is the nursing staff who has to follow up on the doctors' directions. The nurses were Davie's real life-support systems. They watched to be sure his heart was beating properly. They made sure the intravenous needles were feeding the correct amount of fluids into his body. They made sure he was breathing. They kept the wounds clean and the pain levels manageable. I would fight many wars with the nurses, but I knew they were the ones who held on to life for my son twenty-four hours a day.

For a moment the nurse stood staring at the portable tape player stuck in among the intensive-care monitoring systems. She stood listening to the music drown out the metallic sounds of the monitors inside and the PA system outside David's hospital room. Then she looked down at David. He couldn't smile. He couldn't wink. He couldn't con her with his boyish pleas. But his whole body was twisted slightly toward those wonderful, happy sounds. His nurse shrugged and began to sing.

There is just one moon and one golden sun
and a smile means friendship to ev'ry one,
Though the mountains divide

67

and the oceans are wide,
It's a small world after all.

Soon, everyone in that room joined in the song.

It's a small world after all,
It's a small world after all.
It's a small world after all.
It's a small, small world.

From that moment, David had music in his room. We kept it playing almost twenty-four hours a day. Listening to those familiar, happy sounds kept David's mind active. The music helped drown out his fears. It was the only thing I knew to do to help him in his struggle for life, to help him not let go and simply give up. I was afraid that David might die from fear. The music gave him hope that everything was going to be okay.

"But things are not okay, Mrs. Rothenberg," Dr. Achauer said later that day. "Time is running out. We desperately need to begin grafting the ninety percent of Davie's body where his skin is almost entirely burned away. Yet we can't work on Davie's burns until his body is stabilized."

Dr. Achauer went on to explain the various ongoing problems that were postponing the grafting surgery. Davie's lungs were still sloughing off the dead, charred tissue. The ventilator was still necessary to force air down through the damaged bronchial tubes. Pouring such quantities of fluids into Davie's body was causing terrible swelling. The doctors were still cutting incisions in the burned areas to relieve the pressure from the swelling just below the hardened tissue. Tubes were still draining his stomach. Catheters were taking away and monitoring what little waste his body could produce in bowels and kidneys. His kidneys threatened to shut down permanently because there wasn't enough fluid in Davie's body to operate adequately. But Davie was still alive. Almost miraculously he had squeaked through each day's crisis.

And though Davie continued to survive each new crisis, the grafting had been delayed too long. It could be postponed no longer.

John and I sat with Dr. Achauer in the waiting room.

"We must start grafting today," Dr. Achauer said. "Davie is still very critical but we need to begin the grafting or we'll never get ninety percent of his body covered with the tiny skin patches we can harvest from the less than ten percent of the body Davie has left."

"Can you use other people's skin to graft?" I asked, not believing there could be any healthy skin on David's body.

"No, only David's skin can be used. His system would reject anybody else's. And he does have some small patches of healthy skin. Davie lay on his left side in the fire and a small area of skin on his left side was not burned as seriously as the rest."

Achauer went on to explain how even the most serious burn victims usually salvage skin that can be used to graft from their scalp or from the soles of their feet, areas of their chest or back, arms or legs, but in Davie's case, the damage was almost 100 percent.

"We have only a tiny patch of healthy skin under Davie's left arm that we can harvest," Dr. Achauer confessed. "We have waited long enough for his body to stabilize. Now we must begin the grafting."

Dr. Achauer's beeper sounded. He was being summoned to surgery. He stood, but he didn't rush away. He looked at me. In a very short time he had tried to explain the grafting process. He had told me how risky any surgery was when Davie was still in such unstable condition. He had tried to warn me that it was a tricky job to graft so large an area from so small a source of healthy skin. He knew there were dozens of questions I wanted to ask, but he also knew there was no more time. I smiled a smile of resignation and shrugged my shoulders.

"Good luck," I said, swallowing hard. He nodded and was gone.

"What day is it?" I asked John, blinking back my tears and feeling really frightened.

"It's Saturday," he answered. "No, Sunday," he corrected, as confused as I was by the stress of those first days.

"Let's go to church," I said, surprising even myself with the idea.

"Davie's going into surgery, Marie," John reminded me. "Don't you want to be here?"

"Of course I want to be here," I answered impatiently, "but there's nothing we can do for Davie now but wait, so why don't we wait in church?"

We had walked slowly down the hall away from the surgery waiting room toward the police command center. Two policemen approached us looking worried.

"Is there a church around here, really close?" I asked Terry Branum, the public-relations officer on our case.

"Sure, Marie," he answered. "There's a little one just around the corner."

"Let's go," I said.

Officer Branum walked to the telephone and made a call. "How's the lobby?" he asked the policeman on duty three floors below. "Tell them the boy is going into surgery," he whispered, "and that we'll have another report late this afternoon."

I sensed the nervousness in Branum's voice. What I didn't realize was that he had been told by one of the members of the surgical team to expect the worst.

"You're the policeman guarding Marie today," the doctor had said to Branum in a quick conversation just minutes before I approached him about a church.

"We're going to be in there for several hours," the surgeon had told the officer. "I'm afraid the boy won't make it. Stick close to John and Marie. They will need you."

Terry Branum led John and me down the hall and into the lobby. A reporter from the *Los Angeles Times* approached me for an interview. I panicked.

"You don't have to talk to anyone now, Marie," Terry whispered, and then turned to talk to the reporter.

It wasn't easy to walk past reporters and cameramen. They wanted information and they deserved it. Davie's story had created growing public interest all around the nation. People were stunned that a father had tried to burn his child to death. They were curious to see how badly David had been burned. They wanted to know if the boy would live or die. Apparently the people who had heard the first announcement of David's story were calling the newspapers and radio and television stations trying to find out what was happening.

"We'll talk later," Branum said firmly to the reporter still trying to get to me past the six-foot, four-inch-tall officer. "This way, Marie.

There's a car waiting." Branum led John and me to the hospital entrance. We were driven by police car about three blocks from the UCI Burn Center. Several carloads of reporters followed us but kept their distance. Terry hurried us up the stairs and into the Catholic Church on Lewis Street.

"We'll sit right there, Terry, at the back of the church," I told the officer. "If anything happens come and get us," I added, not knowing what might be happening to David at that moment but fearing the worst.

Just as we had left the hospital David had been wheeled past us into the operating room. He was asleep. I wondered if I would see him alive again.

Finally we were seated. The congregation had just completed "the kiss of peace." The priest and the people said together, "Lamb of God, you take away the sins of the world: have mercy on us. Lamb of God, you take away the sins of the world: have mercy on us. Lamb of God, you take away the sins of the world: grant us peace." Holding the communion bread in one hand and the chalice of wine in the other, the priest continued the mass: "May this mingling of the body and blood of our Lord Jesus Christ bring eternal life to those who receive it." Then he added, "This is the Lamb of God who takes away the sins of the world. Happy are those who are called to his supper."

I heard him speaking words from the high altar, but I didn't relate to the mystery of the sacraments that day, only to the mystery of my own son on that operating table and what the team of surgeons and nurses were doing to him at that very moment. The priest and the people together said, "Lord I am not worthy to receive you, but only say the word and I shall be healed." But I barely heard them, for the voice of Dr. Achauer still echoed in my brain.

"First, we have to remove the hardened layers of dead, burned skin," Dr. Achauer had explained. "We've cleaned the top layers away already, but for a graft to hold, we must get down to areas where there is life, where blood flows. There are two ways to proceed. We can anesthetize Davie. We can shave and shave away until we get down to bloody tissue, but that procedure is a tricky one. If there is too much bleeding the graft won't take. In Davie's case I'm afraid that option would not be a wise one."

Dr. Achauer had preferred a second option. "We will remove everything immediately right down to Davie's muscle," he had told me. "We

71

will take out all of David's injured skin and fat so that we know for sure we are down to healthy tissue. That will make it easier to graft. It is safer and quicker and there will be less bleeding."

Before receiving communion the priest said quietly, "May the body of Christ bring me to everlasting life. May the blood of Christ bring me to everlasting life."

Even as the priest prepared to pass the sacraments, I pictured the surgeons cutting through David's dead, black skin to the pink, healthy muscle tissues below. There was danger in this radical surgery. Without microscopic surgery, it was difficult to know exactly where dead flesh ended and living flesh began. But there was so much area to cover and such a small patch of healthy donor skin to use in covering it that Dr. Achauer chose the more radical option to cut everything away that was damaged and begin again on a layer below where the graft had a better chance of holding.

As the priest prepared to distribute the communion, the congregation approached the altar railing. He said to each one, "This is the body and blood of Christ" and the communicant replied, "Amen." Was Davie at that very moment receiving his new skin?

Dr. Achauer had showed me the instrument which could roll across that tiny patch under David's arm, cutting away a piece of skin only one-one hundredth of an inch thick. Sue Martinez had demonstrated another tool that cut holes into that healthy skin.

"The mesher makes the tiny piece of freshly harvested skin look like a hair net or a fishing net," she had explained. "It is mainly holes held together by strands of skin. That way the skin can fan out to three times its original size. During grafting in the surgery, Dr. Achauer will drape that net of skin over an area of David's body that has been prepared to receive it. Then we watch as that skin begins to grow and to replace the old skin."

The choir was singing in the balcony just behind us. People were still lining up to receive communion. I didn't move. I just sat there. The priest was saying over and over again, quietly to each believer, "This is the body and blood of Christ."

"Life comes up from beneath the graft," Dr. Achauer had explained. "The tiny blood vessels circulating blood throughout David's system sense the grafted skin and begin immediately to grow toward it. The blood vessels below hook up with the blood vessels in Davie's graft.

Quickly, the two vascular systems become one again, and blood flows through those tiny strands of skin. As blood flows the network becomes alive. The skin gradually creeps across the surface until it meets other skin. Then it grows in another direction entirely. It can only grow about an inch, but if you have two pieces of skin two inches apart and each side grows an inch in each direction, they will eventually meet. Then David will have a new skin and a new chance at life."

As I accepted the gift of Christ's body for new life, I pictured David receiving his new skin. As I accepted the gift of Christ's blood for new life, I pictured donor's blood flowing into David to replace the blood he would lose in surgery. I stood before the altar. My eyes filled with tears. My hands trembled. "For new life," the priest had said, and I prayed a desperate prayer that what was happening at that moment would be enough new life for both of us.

The mass had ended. The final choral anthem had been sung. We joined the others standing to receive the final blessing:

"Lord we give thanks for these holy mysteries which bring to us here on earth a share in the life to come. Grant this through Christ our Lord."

"Amen," said the congregation.

"Go in the peace of Christ."

"Thanks be to God."

As we left the church, we saw Officer Branum sitting in his police car waiting for the radio to bring the bad news he had been prepared to receive. There was no news from the operating room, good or bad. We drove back to the hospital in silence. Finally, John spoke.

"You know, Marie," he began quietly, "I have to head back to New York tomorrow."

"I know," I answered, not knowing what I would do without him. Soon I would be commuting alone by police car between the Holiday Inn and the UCI Burn Center. I would have only occasional friends or family to stand with me at David's bedside. I didn't know if I would lose my job. I didn't know how I would pay the medical bills which would run into hundreds of thousands of dollars. And now John, my fiancé, had to leave me to go back to his job as a policeman in New York City, three thousand miles away.

Again Officer Branum escorted us through the lobby, which was even more packed with media people now waiting for news from the doctors after David's first major surgery. We walked through the intensive-care unit without speaking. As we turned to enter the waiting room, Ken and Judy Curtis stood up to greet us. I hugged Judy tightly.

"How is he?" I asked no one in particular.

"They are just finishing surgery," Ken answered. "Dr. Achauer should be here any minute."

"When are you going back to New York?" Ken asked John casually as we waited for Dr. Achauer to bring us news.

"Soon," John answered under his breath, hoping I wasn't listening.

"Too soon," I added, feeling miserable.

"Why don't you come and stay with us?" Judy asked. "We have plenty of room."

I couldn't believe what they were saying. Only a few days before we were total strangers. At that point we had known each other for about three days, yet Ken and Judy were inviting me to move in with them.

"I couldn't," I answered abruptly. "Thank you anyway, but we have no idea how long this is going to be."

"It doesn't matter to us," Judy said. "Stay as long as you need to."

Just at that moment, Dr. Achauer strode across the waiting room. "The graft is in place," he said, "and Davie got through the surgery without incident."

"Thank God," Ken whispered.

"Amen," Judy joined in.

Dr. Achauer looked at the two of them for a moment, then back at me. "But there is a long way to go, Marie," he warned. "There are so many other things that could go wrong, we just don't know what will happen or when."

"Will he make it?" I asked, begging Dr. Achauer for information he could not give.

"I wish I could tell you," he answered, moving toward me. "But I can't. In a few days I can tell you if the graft is holding. I can tell you now that the antibiotics seem to be fighting off the bacterial infections. David's kidneys seem to be working well. The fluids in his body are beginning to balance and the swelling is going down. The lungs are already beginning to heal themselves. We have one catheter monitoring his heart and another his lungs. Now, we just work and wait."

The minute Dr. Achauer finished his report, Ken and Judy invited us all to join hands and pray with them again. Dr. Achauer excused himself and headed down the hall, looking back over his shoulder at us. We stood in the hallway, holding hands, our heads bowed.

"We thank You, Lord," Judy said, "for David and for his doctors and nurses and the way they are working together with You in the miracle of David's healing. . . ."

I opened my eyes as Judy continued to pray. I couldn't believe I was standing there in the hall, holding hands and praying. Who were these people? Why did I feel so wonderful when they appeared? Were they from some cult? Were they out to get something from me? Did they want to benefit from David's publicity?

"Sometimes it is hard, Lord," Judy was praying, "to believe in You when things go bad. But that is the time we need You most. Help Marie, Lord, and John. . . ."

I could see the tears streaming down Judy's face. Ken gripped my hand, his eyes closed tightly, his face furrowed in concern for David. They both seemed so sincere. I knew from experience that the people who seem most sincere are the ones you need to mistrust the most. So I held back. I heard the prayer and was grateful for it, but I tried to keep my perspective about those who prayed that prayer.

"Amen."

Ken and Judy looked up at us, smiling. They smiled all the time. They were positive and loving and generous and scary.

"Remember, Marie, we really want you to come stay with us. We have plenty of room and we would love to share it."

The moment they were out of sight I began to worry out loud to John.

"I don't want to move into their home," I said, frightened.

"Why not?" John asked. "They really seem like nice people."

"John, what if they are connected with some cult?" I said.

"What?" John's mouth opened in surprise. He looked at me, unbelieving.

"I mean it. This is California. Remember Jim Jones? That's the way he got people to follow him. He seemed so nice but just below the surface he was nuts, a killer."

"I don't think Ken and Judy are nuts or killers or from some cult, Marie."

"Well, what if they are connected with Charles in some way?"

"Charles?" John walked me toward the hall. "You need to get out of this place for a while," he said worriedly. "You are cracking up."

We walked and talked for hours. I needed to accept Ken and Judy's invitation. The motel bills over the next few months would be into the thousands of dollars. I didn't even know yet whether or not insurance would cover Davie's hospital stay, which was costing more than three thousand dollars per day. I had nothing in my savings account in Brooklyn and there were no parents or grandparents, in-laws or outlaws, waiting in the wings to pay the bills.

"What if they are connected with Charles?" I asked again. "I don't know these people."

"How could they be?" John argued. "Charles doesn't have friends here, not like Ken and Judy."

"I don't know them," I argued back. "And Charles is just crazy enough to have paid two crazy friends to get me alone in their house. I'll get there and they'll try to kill me like Charles tried to kill David."

"Marie, your imagination is running away with you. Slow down. Think."

We talked to the policemen who had guarded us at the hotel. We talked to the nurses. We talked to each other.

"What if they are murderers?" I asked.

"Murderers don't follow you around praying, Marie," a detective answered. "They seem like nice people."

"Besides, they don't know any more about you than you know about them," a nurse added. "Maybe you're a murderer or a thief. Seems to me *they're* taking the risk."

That thought had occurred to me. Perhaps the best proof of Ken and Judy's sincerity was that they were taking a chance on me. Not many people had ever taken a chance on me. The next morning I called Judy to accept her invitation, but I had a plan to keep down the risk.

"Judy, if you still want me, I'd like to stay with you but only for a week."

"Oh, wonderful," she said. I could hear her family cheering in the background. "Stay as long as you want."

"But there is one more problem," I added. "My brother Rich is flying in to visit David. I would like him to spend the first night with me. Would that be okay?"

"Of course," Judy answered. "We have room for Richard, too."

I placed the phone back on the detective's desk. "Well, I did it," I said. "I sure hope this isn't another big mistake."

Innocently, I had sent my son off to his near death. Now I was placing my own life in the hands of strangers. I don't know if anybody from Southern California can understand how difficult it is for a New Yorker to move into a stranger's house. In Brooklyn we hardly see the inside of a neighbor's house after living next door for years. I unlock my apartment's safety locks, put my collar up against the cold, walk quickly through darkened neighborhoods frightened by every strange sound, every quick movement. I wait for the subway in darkened tunnels deep beneath the street. I ride in silence with hundreds of other people whose collars are up against the cold and against each other. I work. I return to my apartment. I relock the safety locks and wait for another day to begin.

We are alone even in a crowded subway car or busy city street. It is too big a risk to look someone in the eye who may pass you on the street. It is too big a risk to begin a friendly conversation with a stranger. It is too big a risk to accept an invitation from anybody you don't really know. And Ken and Judy popped into my life, looked me in the eye, and asked me to stay with them. It was a shock and I was afraid.

Another Southern California couple had called to offer me a car. I couldn't believe that, either. Peg and Ken Schmidt drove three hours that day to loan me their second car. "For as long as you need it," they said. In Brooklyn I couldn't even catch a cab.

At 9:00 P.M. that evening, my brother Rich arrived at the hospital from the airport. Ken and Judy met us in front of the hospital to lead us in my borrowed car to their home. It was raining. We drove for several miles over twisting, hillside roads above Fullerton.

"Where are they taking us, Richie?" I asked, growing more frightened. We were high above the city. The houses thinned out. There were no street lights. The road was dark and narrow.

"This doesn't look good, Richie," I said. "It's like something out of an Alfred Hitchcock movie."

Suddenly, Ken drove his car through large iron gates. We followed down a private drive to a rambling ranch-style home with a Spanish tile roof.

"Oh, Richard. I don't think I'm going to like it here. It's too rich for me. How did these people get a house like this, anyway?"

Rich just kept smiling. "Don't worry, Marie. You can always move out."

We parked the car on a sweeping circular driveway. Ken and Judy's kids, Greg, twenty, and Melanie, sixteen, were standing on the porch with an umbrella to greet us. Judy's mother stood just behind them. They hugged us and hurried us in out of the rain.

The house was huge. My entire apartment could fit in the family room. Through the windows I could see a lighted swimming pool and a large fountain. There was stained glass and oil paintings, a pool table, and a huge video console. We walked through the entryway past a staircase that curved up to the bedrooms upstairs. There were so many rooms the house seemed never-ending.

"You could get lost in this house," I mumbled to myself.

"What's that?" Judy asked.

"Pretty house," I said.

"Your bedroom is upstairs," Judy said as she led me toward the stairway. "And Rich can sleep downstairs in the guest room."

"Oh, no," I almost pleaded with her. "I want to be near my brother tonight." I was so afraid in that big house with this crowd of strangers that I almost began to cry.

"We have a room for you upstairs, Marie," Judy was smiling. "You need a place where you can get away and be alone. We'll leave the lights on in the hallway. Any time you get afraid, you can come right down the stairs to Richard."

After cake and ice cream and coffee, I walked up the circular staircase to my room. Ken and Judy had built a two-bedroom apartment upstairs for Judy's mother, Grandma June, who was glad to share her space with me. I had my own bath, access to a little kitchen, a beautiful four-poster bed, a television set, and a whole library of religious books to read.

I lay in that bed listening to the storm outside the window. The leaves and shrubbery were banging against the wall. Wind rattled the windows and rain ran noisily down the windowpane. I got out of bed and stared out the window into the darkness, and I was genuinely afraid. Davie had almost died on a California night just like this one, in a motel only a few miles away. I began to imagine that this night would be my night to die.

They're going to kill me in the night. My ex-husband probably hired them to kill me, I thought.

I opened the closet door slowly. I looked under the bed. I walked around the room. I was terrified. I tested the door. The hall lights were on. I remember thinking, *Would a killer build an apartment for his mother-in-law?*

"God, please protect me through this night," I prayed, as I got back into bed. "And protect David in the hospital."

Still praying desperate, frightened prayers, I finally fell asleep.

7

I awakened early the next morning in that huge house on the hill. I was glad for the California sunshine streaming in the window. The rain had washed the world free of smog, and clouds passing between the sun and me left dancing patterns on the floor and ceiling of the room. The house was alive with voices. I could hear music playing, and I could smell freshly brewed coffee.

Quickly I dressed and walked down the stairway looking for my brother. He was seated at the kitchen table drinking coffee and talking with Ken as if they were old friends. I wanted to run out of that house. I was uncomfortable being there. This was somebody else's home and I felt awkward and out of place.

Ken and Judy both walked toward me. Judy had a cup of tea brewed and offered it to me. Ken pulled out the chair beside my brother and seated me. They were treating us like royalty, but instead of feeling glad and grateful, I wondered what they were up to.

"Good morning, Marie," Judy said, smiling.

"Good morning, Marie," Melanie echoed as she ran through the kitchen on her way to Whittier Christian High School. She was wearing a cheerleader's outfit.

"Don't forget your Bible study tonight, Melanie," Judy reminded her daughter as she kissed Ken and headed out the door.

"Have you seen my video tapes, Dad?" Greg asked as he entered the room. "Good morning, Marie," he added. "How did you sleep?"

"I slept fine," I said, drinking my tea and looking about the room. There was an antique barber chair near the pool table, and a wall of family pictures.

Ken was a contractor. There were two different phone systems and sometimes all the phones seemed to be ringing at once. I suppose Judy could see how overwhelmed I was by their home.

"We just about lost this place during the past twelve months," Judy said, sitting down beside me.

"How come?" I asked.

"Ken was burned three months ago," Judy explained. "Just prior to his accident, our business had been down. The building boom had ended. It took every cent to keep the business going and the household running.

"When Ken was burned, we were afraid that we would lose everything. Ken had just gotten out of the hospital. He still couldn't work. The bills were piling up and we were wondering if we could keep this lovely big house that we had built together."

"So what happened?" my brother asked.

"God came to the rescue," Judy said, smiling.

I always blinked hard when she spoke of God so easily, as though He were a friend or a neighbor.

"When Ken's clients knew he was back on the job, we began to pick up work. And to tide us over until we were paid for the new jobs, the church held a jogathon to raise money to help pay the old bills."

"A what?" I asked.

"A jogathon," she answered.

"In fact, the jogathon was held the day we met you," Ken remembered. "They marked a track around our church parking lot. Sixty or seventy people got hundreds of other people to sponsor them at so much money per lap.

"They raised fifteen thousand dollars to help us through our crisis," Judy said.

"Everybody was running," Greg chimed in. "Even Chuck Swindoll."

"It was kind of comical," Ken added. "Rod Hoschouer, our associate pastor, ran up to me after doing seventy laps and said, 'I think I ran the most laps, Ken.'

" 'How many did you run?' somebody asked him.

" 'Seventy laps,' he answered proudly, still gasping for air.

" 'Gee, Rod, I'm sorry to tell you this,' someone else chimed in, 'but

Chuck Swindoll ran more than seventy-five laps and he left fifteen minutes ago.' "

As Ken finished his story, Judy and Greg joined in the laughter. I didn't know Chuck Swindoll was a famous pastor with books on *The New York Times* best-seller list. I couldn't understand why a church would hold a jogathon to rescue a family from a crisis. I couldn't believe hundreds of friends and neighbors would spend a morning running to help a family in need. These people were different. It was all so new to me.

"What kind of church is it?" my brother asked and I froze, expecting to hear some obscure cult named.

"We are members of the Eastside Christian Church," Ken answered. "It's on the corner of State College and Yorba Linda Boulevards here in Fullerton."

"How did you get burned?" my brother asked, seeing Ken's scars.

"We were coating a bowling alley with liquid that strengthens and beautifies wood," Ken explained. "The alley was open twenty-four hours a day, so we started the job at midnight hoping to miss the crowds. The manufacturer of the coating liquid assured us that it was nonflammable. In fact, they provided a propane torch to help speed up the drying.

"A worker was drying the area at one end of the alley and I was coating the other end. Suddenly the fumes ignited. The entire area burst into flames. A wall of fire rolled over me. I was standing in flames. My clothes were burning. I ran toward the lobby of the bowling alley trying to rip my flaming clothing off as I ran. At the same time I was yelling for someone to help. A woman who was bowling nearby knocked me down and managed to throw something over me and snuff out the flames. Ten minutes later the paramedics were there pouring saline solution all over me. An ambulance rushed me to the Sherman Oaks Burn Center. I was there off and on for the next two months."

"I think I should go to the hospital to see Davie," I interrupted. "Richie, are you ready?"

My brother excused himself and we hurried from the house.

"What's wrong, Marie?" he asked me. "You seemed so restless in there."

"I am restless. I can't figure out those people."

"They're just being nice," he assured me.

"Too nice," I added. "Why would they invite me to move in with them when they have enough troubles of their own?"

We twisted back down those roads in silence, Richard following the map Judy had drawn and I marveling at the beauty of the homes and gardens in the hills of Southern California. I led Richard up the back stairs of the UCI Medical Center Burn Center into the intensive-care unit where Davie would be waiting.

"Good morning, Marie," Terry Branum said when he saw me.

"Marie, the press is here en masse," he warned. "You are going to have to say something pretty soon."

"I can't talk to TV cameras," I protested. "I don't know what to say. Can't *you* tell them how Davie is doing?"

"They all want to interview *you*, Marie," he answered.

"I can't, Terry. I'm too nervous."

Sue Martinez, the head nurse, passed us on her rounds. "Can I see David now?" I asked, hoping he was back from his morning trip to the bath.

"He's almost ready, Marie," she answered. "By the time you get suited, he'll be waiting."

"How is he?" I asked her.

"He's doing okay," she said, choosing her words slowly. "The graft looks good. His coughing has slowed. They're going to do another bronchoscopy today to see how the lungs look. His vital signs are strong. I'm encouraged."

Richard and I excused ourselves from Terry and walked into the dressing area to put on gowns and masks. I finished first and entered David's room.

"Good morning, Davie," I said, not knowing whether he was asleep or awake. He turned his head to one side. Those strange gurgling sounds came up out of his throat again.

"Don't try to talk yet, Davie," I said, sitting down beside him. "Everything is all right. What about some music?"

He nodded slowly. I put on the tape still loaded in the machine. It was a children's choir. They were singing about Jesus. I looked closely at the tape and saw the name "Children's Choir, Eastside Christian Church. Greg Curtis." Judy and Ken had left the tape. The room was filled with children's voices. "Jesus loves the little children," they sang, "all the children of the world." David settled back against the pillow and listened. I turned from the tape deck and walked over to my son. It was then that I noticed. Davie was lying fully exposed on the open bed. He had been bathed and white ointment covered his body except where the grafting had been done. That area had turned completely black.

I moved to take a closer look. There was no mistake. His arm and leg were black. Gangrene!

I ran from the room. "Davie's turned black!" I shouted at the first nurse who passed. "Do something. His arm looks like it's falling off."

I was in a panic. Dee Fraser, one of Davie's nurses, rushed up.

"What's the matter, Marie?" she asked.

"What's the matter?" I echoed, steering her across the room. "David's arm and leg are black. They'll have to be amputated. Sue said the grafting went well. Look at him."

The nurse turned to look at Davie. Then she looked back at me, trying hard not to laugh.

"That's cadaver skin," she said, and then began to laugh.

"Cadaver skin?" I whispered.

"When an area of the body has been debrided, Marie, the doctor protects the uncovered area with skin from a cadaver."

"A cadaver?" I asked again. "You mean somebody else's skin? Somebody dead?"

"That's right," she nodded. "The doctor is preparing Davie for grafting. After the dead skin has been cut away, the newly cleaned area must be protected from organisms in the air. So the cadaver skin is placed over the area and held in place with large sterile staples until it is not needed."

"Why is it black?" I asked, whispering so Davie wouldn't hear.

"Because the donor's skin was black, Marie."

I stared at David. He was wrapped in somebody else's skin. That person happened to be black. I didn't know if it was a black man, woman, or child. I just knew that my son was being saved because someone else's son or daughter had died.

Music filled the room. "Jesus loves the little children. All the children of the world. Red and yellow, black and white, They are precious in His sight. Jesus loves the little children of the world."

I stayed with Ken and Judy Curtis and their family the entire time Davie was in the UCI Burn Center. Every morning there was water heated, a tea bag and cup on the kitchen stove. There was fresh fruit and a bowl for one of the dozen or so varieties of cereals Judy had ready to pamper every taste. Ken and Judy never accepted money for their hospitality. I did try to pay them.

"I want to pay you one hundred dollars a week," I insisted one evening during those first few days at the Curtis home. "That will help a little with the extra expenses I cause your family."

"I can't take money from you, Marie," Judy insisted.

"But the room is so nice and you do so much to make my life pleasant. At one hundred dollars I'm still saving a lot of money."

Judy led me to a chair, placed another cup of tea in my hands, and sat down across the table from me.

"Marie, we aren't doing this for money, you know," she said.

"Of course," I assured her. "I know that, but—"

"We're doing this because we want to help, because it gives us pleasure to help you."

"No," I insisted stubbornly, "you must take it. I can't stay here unless you do. I have to feel like I'm giving you something in return. I just can't take from you like that."

Judy started to argue. Then she changed her mind. "Okay, I'll take the money. We'll put it right here in the food closet. And we'll use it when we need it."

I thought I had won. The next evening, upon my return from the hospital, I walked into my room and discovered that Judy had used the money after all. There was a wonderful flannel nightgown and slippers so that I could walk around the house without getting dressed. There was a lightweight blouse and skirt for California weather. I had arrived in Buena Park with only the clothes on my back. Judy had shopped well.

"Marie," Judy called from downstairs. "There's a call for you."

Terry Branum was calling from the hospital. "Marie, the press are getting restless. They are calling here from all over the world to speak to you about David. You have to say something pretty soon."

"But Terry," I argued, "you are the press officer. You have the experience in talking to reporters and TV crews. I don't. It scares me."

"They don't want to hear from me, Marie. They want to hear from you."

"Well, how can I talk to them all? I need to spend the time with Davie."

"I have an idea," he said. "Let's invite them to the Buena Park police station. I'll put them in our media room. I'll bring you in for ten minutes, sit you down, and let them ask questions. After a few minutes, you leave. Everybody will be happy."

I had been in Southern California for almost a week. The press had been wonderful. As they told Davie's story, people wrote or called or telegraphed their concern. The cards and letters had checks and bills folded and stuffed into the envelopes. "To help with Davie," they said. Several thousand dollars had come in. I owed the press an interview. But those next two days dragged by painfully. I was so afraid of standing up before the press and trying to answer their questions about Charles and Davie. I became more and more nervous. As the time for the Friday press conference came closer I wasn't sure I could go through with it. I called Terry Branum.

"Officer Branum, please," I asked the Buena Park dispatcher.

"Officer Branum, here," he responded.

"Terry, this is Marie."

"You aren't going to chicken out on me, are you, Marie?" he asked.

"No, I'll be there in two hours just as I promised. Ken and Judy are bringing me down, but I need something to calm my nerves."

"Like what?" he asked.

"Like Valium or something that will relax me."

"Valium?" he asked. "We don't have any Valium down here."

"Well, it's a police department isn't it?" I answered. "You have to have Valium around there somewhere."

"Marie," Terry explained, with only the slightest hint of exasperation, "the only drugs we have down here are locked away as evidence, but I'll see what I can do."

Apparently Terry called his wife to see if she had any Valium. She had recently been in a car accident and a doctor had prescribed a muscle relaxant. She gave two of the large red pills to Terry. He brought them to the station just as we arrived.

The police station was surrounded by remote trucks with receiving dishes. Technicians rushed about in a frenzy of preparation. Cameras and lights and microphones were everywhere. The room was filling up with reporters. I took one look inside that room and panicked.

"You've got to find something to calm me," I demanded.

Terry appeared with the pills and a glass of water. "I don't know what these things are," he said, "but my wife says a half of one should do it." I gulped down a whole pill and walked into Terry's office to await my first conference with the press. After a few minutes, the room began to weave back and forth. I could hardly stand.

"Terry," I said, searching for him with my eyes half-closed.

"Yes, Marie," he answered, looking down at the list of questions he had prepared for my briefing.

"Terry, I'm going to faint," I said.

"What?" He ran across the room to me. "Those pills. What have they done to you?"

"I don't know," I said, smiling and weaving about, "but I don't feel nervous anymore."

Slowly, Terry led me through that crowd of reporters. I felt no pain.

Voices echoed slightly. Everyone seemed far away. I smiled. The press smiled back. I was relaxed from the medication and totally at ease.

"I just want to be here a few minutes," I said, whispering through my smile. "Just a few minutes, remember."

"Okay," Terry answered. "I'll introduce you. Do a few questions. And when you get tired, just slap my knee under the table and I'll say 'Okay, folks, that's it for now. Marie's tired. Thank you for coming.'"

I nodded. It was a good plan. Only that big red pill kept the plan from working.

"Ladies and gentlemen," Terry began. "I would like to introduce Marie Rothenberg, David's mom."

Several reporters stood and one by one the questions were asked. I told David's whole story up to that point. I described my vigil in a small, third-floor hospital room at the UCI Burn Center. I tried to help them understand what it meant to watch my six-year-old child fight for his life.

"He can't see or speak," I told them, "but I never run out of things to talk to him about. I tell him that I love him a thousand times a day."

They asked if I thought he should live with such terrible burns. I confessed how difficult that decision had been for me.

"At first," I told them, "I thought it might be better if David died. But he's fought so hard. He fights to live every day. He's got a right to live. Watching him struggle gives me strength to go on living myself."

They asked about David's progress. "Some days are good," I answered, "last night was bad. All the graphs, the monitors started going crazy. I thought I might lose him. But today has been a good day."

"What do you do all day?" a reporter asked.

"I stay in his room from eight o'clock in the morning until ten in the evening. I leave him only when he takes his daily whirlpool bath or undergoes a treatment or surgery. I read him passages from his favorite book, *The Little Engine That Could,* or lines from the two thousand cards and letters we have already received. Sometimes I ask if he wants me to read and he shakes his head no."

When they asked me what had been the most difficult part of our ordeal to date, I answered, "When David feels the pain, and he feels so much pain every day, that hurts me most. I cannot take his pain away, I cannot even share it."

They asked me about my ex-husband, Charles. "I don't feel the bitterness right now. It's not my place to judge him or to hate him. He will have to live with this for the rest of his life, but I don't understand it. . . . If he wanted to hurt me," I wondered aloud, "why didn't he try to kill me?"

"Excuse me for asking, Mrs. Rothenberg," a reporter began, "but does David know his father was the person who burned him?"

It was a question we had to face. I had worried about the moment David would want to know. Now the press were wondering, too.

"I don't want to tell him right away," I spoke quietly in response. "David doesn't understand what happened to him and I don't want to hurt him anymore."

"What will happen to David now?" someone asked.

"The doctors say that if he makes it through the next few weeks, he will require years of surgery and therapy to mobilize his joints, to repair his hands, and to rebuild his face."

Then I saw Ken and Judy sitting with the press smiling confidently at me. I remembered the talks we had had about Davie's future and entrusting him into the hands of God. I continued talking to the press.

"I have to leave Davie's future in God's hands now. The doctors and nurses are doing everything possible to save him. I have to take one day at a time. There isn't much need to worry about the future until we get through the present. And God and our new friends are helping us get there."

People asked questions. I answered them. I felt more and more talkative as I warmed up. My answers got longer and longer. Terry had been expecting me to slap his knee after the first five or six minutes. I was still talking thirty minutes later.

Whatever was in that pill was wonderful. I have a feeling it's what politicians take before they meet the press.

We returned to the UCI Burn Center. The calming effect of the pill was wearing off. I gowned immediately and went into Davie's room.

"Hi, Davie," I whispered. "Mommy's back. Are you feeling okay?"

David was listening to music from a children's album on David and Goliath. He nodded at me. He was still on the respirator. He couldn't speak. He couldn't see. He could hardly shift his body in his bed. He felt great pain, and as I watched him lying there I wondered what awful fears must go through his mind. His brain had not been damaged—at least no one thought it had. He was a smart kid. He knew something terrible *had* happened and something terrible *was* happening to him, but he couldn't ask questions. Doctors and nurses rushed about but no one stopped to explain to him, or to me, what was going on.

In the early evening when Davie returned from his bath, I noticed that one of his ears had fallen off. A night nurse was just entering. "What happened to David's ear?" I asked.

"I really don't know, Mrs. Rothenberg," she said, placing items on David's tray and not even looking in his direction. "This is the first night I've taken care of David. You'll have to ask the doctors." Her answer seemed so heartless.

Patients and their family and friends need information. I understand how little extra time doctors and nurses have to sit down with those concerned and explain the treatment day by day. But we have the right to understand what is being done to those we love. The patients, too, have the right to know.

I stared one long, angry stare at the night nurse, then ran into the hallway. Another doctor on David's case, Dr. Sankary, was standing not far away. I called to him from the doorway of Davie's room.

"I want to talk to you about David's ear," I said, interrupting his conversation with another doctor. All my relaxed controls from the press conference were gone. All the pent-up fear and frustration of the past few weeks just boiled up in me. It was a battle—the rights of patients and their families versus the rights of the medical community. I felt as if I were unraveling. I was talking about Davie's ears, but I was feeling the accumulated rage and helplessness and exhaustion of too many twenty-four-hour days, too much shock, too much stress, and too much anger.

"Why don't you calm down, Marie," Dr. Sankary said, walking toward me, "and let's talk about it away from Davie's door. It isn't good for him to hear this."

I felt embarrassed and put down, but I knew Davie shouldn't hear me shouting. I stuck my head inside the room. "Davie, I'm going to speak to the doctor for a moment. I'll be right back."

We walked a few paces down the hall; then my voice rose again. "I want to know what happened to David's ears!"

"What has happened, Marie?" he asked innocently. *As if he didn't know,* I thought to myself. "David's left ear has fallen off and you don't even know it?" I shouted, my anger rising.

"You don't seem to understand," he began, "that with such serious burns, there is a very strong possibility this will happen."

"Strong possibility?" I echoed. "Are you telling me that you knew all along that Davie's ears could fall off and you didn't even tell me?"

The doctor looked embarrassed. For a moment he turned away. I followed him, my finger waving in his face, my voice loud and strident.

"I want to ask you something," I began. "David is not your first burn patient, is he?"

I waited. The doctor didn't respond.

"Well," I asked again, "is David your first burn patient or not?"

"No, Marie, of course not," he answered, resigned to the attack about to follow.

"Then you have some experience in these things, correct?" I asked angrily.

"Yes, Marie," he answered again.

"You are the doctor. I am the mother. You know what the possibilities are in my son's case. I don't. When you have even the slightest idea that something could happen to him, you tell me before it happens. Next time, if you know there is a possibility that Davie will lose an ear or two, you'd better tell me, because my son's ears, like everything else about him, are important to me. I do not want to be surprised like that again."

The doctor looked tired. I continued my attack.

"Tell me now what's going to happen to David next," I demanded. "Will he lose his eyes? Will his nose fall off? What about his fingers or his toes? Can I be sure they'll be on his hands and feet in the morning?"

I knew Dr. Sankary was an excellent physician. I knew, too, that he and the entire medical team were struggling to save Davie's life and they had little time to keep me informed about the process. But they could do a better job of it, or I would know the reason why.

"I don't expect to go out and buy a burn book or a medical encyclopedia to look up the possibilities, doctor," I shouted. "That is your job. And I expect you to come and tell me. I don't want to go into my son's room every day with a magnifying glass to see what is missing next."

"All right, Marie, I'm sorry," he said.

I wasn't finished. "It is your job to tell me what might happen to my son. I want to know. Is he going to lose anything else? Are there any more surprises?"

"Marie," he answered more firmly, "there are some families who don't want to know. They're not like you. They're afraid. They just want to be told when it's over, one way or the other."

"Well," I answered, "I want to know what could happen to my son and I want to know before it happens. I can't take this bit-by-bit business. It's tearing me apart. Let me know once and for all so that I can get over the shock, accept it, and go about the business of helping my boy survive."

The doctor took my hand and let me yell at him.

"I want to know everything now. I don't want to walk out of this hospital every day with a part of me missing. Help me know and understand the possibilities. I want to prepare myself to face them so that I can help Davie face them, too."

The doctor spoke honestly. "You are obviously a strong woman, Marie," he began. "And I assure you that from now on you will have a daily report."

"And I don't want to have to chase you people around," I added. "I'll be here when you have news. Find me. After you've made your morning visit to my son, tell me if he's making progress or if he's dying. Tell me if he's improved or if he's going down the drain. I don't want to come in here and have to guess. I do not want to be surprised like that again."

I was screaming at him. People were staring as they rushed by. I couldn't stop my angry outburst. Finally, Dr. Sankary took my arms and began to speak.

"Marie," he said, waiting for me to calm down, "Marie, I apologize."

I stood staring at him. My hands were shaking. I felt like throwing up.

"I apologize," he said one more time, trying to get past my defenses and be heard. "And I assure you," he said slowly, calmly, "that from this day we will try to see that you are not surprised again."

The minute he was gone, I returned to David's room. I had promised him one last visit that night. I wanted to break my promise, to run from that intensive-care unit, to find a place to hide. I was so afraid. What would happen next to my poor child? What more would he suffer? But I couldn't leave him without one last visit. I was always afraid that he would die, especially in the night. I hated to leave him alone in his room even for an hour. But the nurses insisted that I get some rest. So, at the end of every long day, I visited David one last time, and this night would be no exception. Conscious or unconscious, sleeping or awake, he would get a visit from his mommy. I never left the hospital without leaning down over him and whispering into his ear, "Good night, Davie. I love you very much." Now that little ear was gone. But he could still hear me, and ear or no ear I would whisper it again. "I am praying for you, son. Sleep well and remember that I love you."

I found my borrowed car in the parking lot and drove those strange new streets to my borrowed room in Ken and Judy's home. I unlocked the front door and rushed toward the stairs to my room.

"Marie?"

Judy and Ken were sitting at the kitchen table waiting up for me. I ran past the stairway and into the kitchen. I was angry and sobbing. Ken jumped up to help me to a chair. Judy already had a cup of tea poured for me.

"What's happened?" she asked. "Is Davie okay?"

"His ear fell off," I said, "and I had to be the one who discovered it."

Ken took my hand. Judy put the tea in front of me and then sat down beside us.

"Why don't they tell me what might happen next?" I began. "It was such a shock. I walked into Davie's room. I bent down to whisper in his ear that everything was going to be all right. And then I discovered his ear was gone. Why didn't they warn me?"

I tried to drink a sip of tea but I couldn't stop crying. Ken and Judy waited. Then Judy began to pray.

"Lord, You love Marie so much. You feel her pain just now even more than we feel it. You know how much she loves Davie, how badly she wants him to come through this thing in one piece. Now he has lost an ear and we have no idea what else he might lose. Please give her the strength she needs to face the surprises, and give the doctors the good sense and insight to help her know what might happen next."

As Judy prayed, I felt relieved. I was glad I had shouted at the doctor on duty. I was grateful for the doctor's apology and for his promise that they would try to keep me better informed about the possibilities. And I was grateful for Ken and Judy, who waited through the night to comfort me.

I lay on my bed a long time before falling asleep. I pictured David in his hospital bed fighting to live, and I begged God to save him and to make him whole and well again.

8

A mug shot of my ex-husband, Charles, appeared on the television screen in my room at Ken and Judy's house in Fullerton. I sat up in bed. Even his picture frightened me. The mug shot held as a newsman said:

A father accused of trying to burn his son to death in a motel room last month waived a preliminary hearing, leading to speculation that he will plead guilty rather than go to trial.

The mug shot dissolved. A live picture of Charles appeared on the screen. He was wearing yellow prison overalls and entering the courtroom of Judge Dave Back, Jr., of the North Orange County Municipal Court in Fullerton.

Fewer than one defendant a year opts to forego a preliminary hearing which determines whether sufficient evidence exists to hold a trial.

Charles sat in the courtoom. His legs were shackled. His hands were bound together. He had a light growth of beard and sat with his shoulders slightly hunched. The reporter continued:

The judge warned Rothenberg that dropping the hearing could have very serious consequences for him. But Rothenberg, who has admitted setting the fire, says he decided to cancel his hearing because he doesn't want to add to the burdens of the people involved.

As I watched my ex-husband sitting there so apparently contrite, I began to shake. I pulled the covers up to close out the cold. The newsman continued talking. He described how Charles had signed over the thirteen thousand dollars in his possession at the time of his capture in San Francisco to David for his medical care. Once again he quoted Charles' accusation that it had been my phone call, "threatening to keep David from him," that led to the attempted murder.

I went downstairs to the kitchen to make myself a cup of tea. Ken and Judy and their family were asleep already. I knew I wouldn't be able to sleep. Charles was out there for all the world to see, asserting his innocence and my guilt, or at least my complicity in his guilt. That fed my fears that one day Davie might blame me for this entire ugly event. I first discovered how this might happen when people on the street asked me, "Why did you marry that creep?" or "Why did you stay with him after your marriage?" or "Why did you allow your husband to take the boy away?"

I tried to explain to them how, in many ways, Charles was a better-than-average father. He was possessed by his love for our son. Charles would hang around David's school building on his days off. He would attend the parent-teacher meetings. When it rained without warning, he would bring David's raincoat and umbrella to the classroom in the middle of the day. He even offered to help the school raise money for various causes. He checked with Davie's teachers about his grades. When David was sick Charles would call the school. He poured great quantities of love on David. He seemed to be a good father. There was no reason to suspect that Charles would one day try to murder his son.

But Charles was also a criminal. He had been arrested almost twenty times, primarily for theft and vagrancy. He had been in jail twice during our short marriage. That he was a thief and a con man was well established. I was suspicious that he was an arsonist as well. Though there is no official evidence, I am still convinced that Charles was responsible for starting the fire that damaged our Laundromat (for the insurance money) and the fire that almost burned our apartment to the ground (for revenge).

For all of us who knew Charles, it was difficult to sort out who he really was: loving father or potential murderer. He lied so much that even he couldn't tell where truth ended and the lie began. I felt guilty for not catching the clues earlier, but I didn't. Others missed them, too.

One reporter interviewed Charles' former employer at the car service in Brooklyn where Charles had worked. "None of us believe he did that to his son," the dispatcher said. "He was crazy about David. He drove all the other drivers crazy talking about his son. He never talked about anything else." The principal of David's school was quoted as saying, "We at PS 58 thought Charles was the perfect father because he never showed us anything else. It was very difficult for any of us in this building to accept what David's father did to David. We knew one man and then he turned around—that must have been difficult for Mrs. Rothenberg also."

Of course it was difficult for me. It took me a long time to discover Charles' dark side. He was attractive, glib, soft-spoken, and loving. When you are a single girl alone in New York and a handsome stranger courts you with roses you don't call the police to ask if he has a record. If I had called I would have found a criminal record as long as my arm.

Then when I began to see Charles' other side I found reasons to excuse him. "Charles was tired," I rationalized, or "Charles was stressed." "Charles needed money and though he stole it he intended to pay it back." "Charles wasn't raised in a good home." "He had no family." At first I made up endless reasons for his strange behavior. But when he was convicted the second time, the excuses ended and I finally found the courage to divorce him.

That wasn't easy. David was only two. I had no money. I had endless bills that Charles had accumulated. Upon his arraignment for grand theft Charles cried in the courtroom and begged me to stay with him. My family said I should give him another chance. But the uneasy feelings I had about Charles piled up until I could go through with the divorce in spite of everyone's disapproval.

Then Charles was about to be released from jail the second time. For months before his release I had felt afraid. My intuition was warning me. We were divorced by then. I wasn't afraid that Charles would hurt David, but I thought he might try to kidnap him, and I was sure he would do everything he could to make my life miserable.

I told my friends I wanted to move away so that Charles couldn't find us. They said, "You can't run away from this situation. He'll find you. Besides, he's David's father. David has a right to see his dad. He'll constantly be asking you where his father is. That wouldn't be fair to Davie."

When I expressed my fears about Charles' release to my family they told me, "Oh, little David is so sad since his father has been in jail. Let him see his daddy again." Then I felt guilty. I started thinking, *Am I doing the wrong thing, trying to keep David from Charles?* Down inside I wanted to take David to some safe and distant place. I didn't want Charles to spoil him again. I didn't want to risk David's being kidnapped. But I never dreamed Charles would try to murder our son.

Now, soon, I would have to tell David what his father had done. It was awful to be seen on television and in the papers almost daily trying to explain. But to tell my son that his daddy had tried to kill him was the worst task I could imagine.

I arrived at the UCI Burn Center late the next morning. Little by little David had regained his sight. He was beginning to see how much damage the fire had caused his body. But he couldn't speak. I was afraid if and when he ever regained the power of speech the first question he would ask would be "Why?"

As I walked into the intensive-care unit, I saw a crowd of nurses gathered around David's door. The doctors had been planning to remove the tubes of the respirator from David's throat. The singed and soot-blackened tissue had been sloughed off. New pink tissue signaled healing. Davie had learned to grunt very understandable commands up around the tubes that were blocking speech. That morning the doctors had removed the obstructions. But when the nurses gathered around to hear him speak, he refused to cooperate.

Sue Martinez approached, grinning broadly. "Come quickly, Marie. We have a surprise for you."

She led me to the gowning area and we quickly pulled masks and gloves in place and headed for the crowd around David's isolation room.

"The doctors took out the respirator tubes this morning," Sue said excitedly.

"Can he talk?" I asked. "What did he say?"

"He refused to speak, Marie," she said, pushing through the crowd.

"Why?" I asked, following her. "What went wrong?"

"Nothing is wrong," she answered. "He wanted to save his first real words for you."

A lump formed in my throat as we worked our way through the crowd waiting to hear Davie's first words.

"Mommy?" he whispered from the bed when he finally saw me.

"Davie. You can talk," I said, tears already streaming down my face.

"Mommy, I'm thirsty," he said.

"Well, get him a drink, somebody," I said through my tears, and the room erupted in applause. Everybody was congratulating him for those words. No one had been sure he would speak again. It was a sign of David's amazing ability to heal. But it was a sign of something more.

Down inside that mass of burned and bleeding tissue, underneath the growing blanket of grafted skin, just behind the layer of ointment and gauze and braces was a child. No longer was he the "burn victim." He was a little boy and he was thirsty. I couldn't believe it. He had been there all the time, but when he didn't speak it was almost as if I couldn't really be sure he was there. Then he spoke. It almost broke my heart. He was really alive and he was talking.

"I want a Coke, Mommy." I wanted to hug him. It was really Davie. Then he ordered lunch—a hamburger and fries. He couldn't have them, of course, not yet. But Davie, the little boy, was back. Everybody in the hospital had been rooting for him. Finally the crowds drifted away and Davie and I were alone. Almost immediately my fears came true.

"What happened to me, Mommy?" he asked.

The television and radio had been off in David's room so that he would not see himself or his daddy on the news. He knew nothing about the fire in room 139 of the Buena Park TraveLodge.

"Davie," I answered him, "I really don't know what happened. You were in a very bad accident."

The doctors agreed that while he was still on the critical list, it would be wise to postpone telling him the details of the fire. I hated to lie, but at that moment it seemed the only thing to do.

"Well, Mommy," Davie continued, "you'd better ask my daddy because he was with me."

Already the wheels were turning inside Davie's brain. I knew he would figure it out sooner or later. I was afraid he would overhear a nurse or a doctor or a policeman in the hall discussing Charles' crime. I was afraid the TV would not stay off forever. I didn't want him to learn about the fire from a stranger. A child psychiatrist in the hospital said, "We have to tell him the truth about the fire, but the truth, at least for now, does not include who set it." I had to trust his advice. So I waited.

One afternoon not long after he said those first words, Davie asked me point-blank, "Where is Daddy, Mommy?"

I paused, searching for the right words. At that moment Charles was in a California prison awaiting final sentencing for his crime. I couldn't lie, but I didn't want to hurt David with the truth.

"How come John can get off work in New York and come all this way to see me," he asked, "but Daddy can't?"

"Daddy is in a place he cannot leave right now," I told him. "And he just can't come to visit even though he wants to."

The psychiatrist and doctors had agreed. David didn't need another trauma. "Keep the truth from him as long as you can." I tried it their way, but David read between the lines. He was only six years old, but he guessed where Charles really was.

"Is Daddy in jail?" he asked.

"David, I don't want to talk about this right now. Let's change the subject and we'll talk about something else."

He painfully leaned forward in his bed.

"I want to know now," he demanded.

I wanted to do the right thing so badly. I couldn't lie. I couldn't tell the truth.

"David, honey," I said walking to the side of his bed. "It's time for sleep. We'll talk about it tomorrow."

I stood beside him for a while. I could see he wanted to talk about his daddy more than anything in the world. But he knew I was as stubborn as he was. So we waited together in silence.

"Good night, David," I said. "I'll see you in the morning."

During the night I lay awake and worried. David was still on the critical list. Dr. Achauer was waiting until the donor area had healed enough to supply new tissue to graft his back. Davie was fighting off one infection after another. He needed all his physical strength to get well. He didn't need this new shock to drain away his energy and his hope. But I couldn't lie any longer. Davie was too smart for that. I couldn't risk losing his trust forever.

At 8:00 A.M. I drove my borrowed car into the UCI Medical Center parking lot. The early-morning sun glared off the pavement. I walked to the Burn Center and took the elevator to the intensive-care unit. About that time, Davie was being lowered into the bath for his daily soak against infection. I gowned slowly. I can still remember pulling on the rubber gloves over each finger, wondering if Davie would insist we begin this morning's conversation where last night's talk had ended. I could see the nurses wheeling David back into his isolation room. I could stall no longer.

"Good morning, Davie," I said. "How was the bath?"

There was silence. Davie lay there looking at me. Finally he spoke. "Mommy," he began. "Did my daddy do this to me?"

I couldn't speak. I just stared at him for a moment. Then he asked again.

"Did he set the hotel on fire?"

I couldn't lie.

"Yes, baby," I stuttered. "He did it."

I suppose he was hoping, as I had hoped, that it wasn't true.

"Why?" he asked, his face beginning to tremble. "Why did Daddy do this to me?"

I began to cry. It was the last thing I wanted to do. I wanted to stand beside him without emotion. I wanted to be able to say the words that would take his pain away. But there was nothing I could say that would help.

"I don't know why, honey. I don't know if we will ever really know why. I know that Daddy loves you Davie, but I can't explain why he did this to you. He was sick. He went crazy. That's all."

David stared at me. Then he, too, began to cry.

"I want to see what my daddy looks like now," he said through his tears. "I want to see his picture."

I had a clipping from the morning paper in my purse describing the crime and Charles' current legal arraignment and the pending trial. It had a recent picture of Charles. I handed the clipping to my son.

"He has a beard?" David asked, staring at the news photo of Charles in the courtroom.

"Yes, he has a beard," I answered. "That's more a five o'clock shadow than a beard," I explained, "but it looks like a beard."

Davie wasn't listening. He was reading the article word for word. I couldn't stop him. He would hear the story from someone. I was glad the reporter had written without sensationalizing it. David read, blinking back his tears.

"What's *arraignment?*" he asked.

"That's when a person accused of a crime stands up before a judge to say whether he is innocent or guilty."

"What did Daddy say?" David asked.

"He said he did it," I answered.

Slowly Davie lay back on his pillow. He clutched the article in one burned hand. He didn't cry. He didn't speak angrily. He just lay there as the awful truth filtered past his defenses and broke his heart.

During the day he asked other questions about the fire.

"Was anyone else hurt?" he asked after a particularly long period of silence.

"No, Davie," I answered. "Why do you ask?"

"Did any other children get burned?" he asked again.

"No," I answered, puzzled by his question. "Why do you ask? The fire only burned your room. Why do you wonder about other children being burned?"

He tried to remember something from that awful night. "Because I heard a baby crying," he explained.

"No," I assured him. "You were the only child hurt, Davie."

"Everybody else was lucky, then," he whispered.

I didn't answer. What could I say?

"Did anyone put shoes on me?" he continued.

I was stunned. David was about to have his fourth major grafting surgery. Dr. Achauer was going to create eyelids that would allow him to shut his eyes for the first time since he was burned. Skin would be grafted to the back of his legs, his right arm, his shoulder, face, and head. Dr. Achauer had explained the procedure to both of us. He had told David that during this surgery, he would also place skin on the soles of his feet.

"Why would you have shoes on?" I asked.

"Because if someone knew I was going to be burned," he answered, "they would have put my shoes on. Then my feet wouldn't have gotten burned and I could walk now."

"Davie," I said, trying desperately not to cry and wanting to take him in my arms. "Nobody knew you were going to get burned. If somebody knew that Daddy was going to do this to you, they wouldn't have let you stay there in the hotel room with him."

Words poured out of me. I tried to explain why no one could have known ahead of time. I tried to tell him how we would have protected him if we had guessed. Six-year-old Davie was trying to understand something no adult will ever fathom.

"I never want to see my dad again," he finally said. Then he began to cry.

I called Ken and Judy. "He's figured it out," I warned them. "I know he would like to see you."

Ken and Judy had visited David faithfully since their first surprise visit. Already he loved them as I did. When I called for help they came immediately. As they entered the room Davie asked me to close the door. He uncrumpled the news clipping about his father's crime.

"Look," he said. "I have a picture of my dad. He's in jail."

Ken moved to David's side. David began to read. He read the article without a mistake. He pronounced every word correctly. He was almost to the end of the article when his voice caught in mid-sentence. He couldn't continue reading. He dropped the article on the bed and began to cry.

Ken and Judy comforted him. I comforted him. During the coming days and nights doctors, nurses, friends and family comforted him. It was not enough.

Davie began to scream at the nurses and the doctors. He was terribly depressed. He cried and he threw tantrums. He refused to even speak to me. I had been the one who told him the bad news. He seemed even more angry at me than at his father. I didn't know what to do with David's rage. I understood it, but I didn't know how to help him deal with it. The anger intensified and seemed to focus. "I hate you!" he screamed at me. "I hate you." He raged and thrashed about in his bed until the nurses were afraid he would cause harm to his own healing process. One afternoon his occupational therapist, Bob Schneider, advised that David's anger should have a more creative outlet than "his poor mother." I agreed.

"Good morning," Bob said, entering David's room the next day.

David took one look at his therapist and began to scream.

"No, no, no!" he said. "Not now. Not today. Not ever."

Bob had been at Davie's side from his first day at UCI Medical Center. He was responsible to keep David's body from contracting. He shaped braces and splints to keep Davie's arms at the proper position during those long, painful nights. His daily exercises often caused David excruciating pain, but David had to exercise or his hands would claw and his body would contract. Just at the climax of his cries of protest, David's psychologist, Lorraine Walsh, entered the room.

"We have a present for you, Davie," she said, holding out a male doll covered in bandages exactly like my son's.

Davie quit screaming protests and looked at the doll. There was an amazing likeness. The little blond doll had a chin splint holding his neck in place. He had hand splints like David's, too, and his hands and arms were bandaged with the stretchy, net gauze that covered David's open wounds. The doll wore elbow splints and leg splints molded carefully to fit his body just like Bob had molded David's splints. And in the kit that accompanied the doll were various items used in David's treatment, including a vicious-looking needle to give shots to his doll like the painful shots David was constantly receiving.

Fascinated, David stared at the little doll. Then he looked at his own body and made the obvious comparisons. Finally, he reached out for it. The psychologist placed the doll on David's outstretched arms. For a moment, he cradled it lovingly. Then he spoke firmly to his occupational therapist.

"Stretch *his* arm," he ordered, "not mine."

From that day, much of David's anger was directed at that poor, long-suffering doll. For the rest of us, it was no small relief.

9

"Sit down, Marie," Dr. Achauer said grimly. "I have to talk to you for a minute."

I already knew that look on Dr. Achauer's face. It meant trouble. I sat down on one of the yellow plastic chairs in the waiting room.

"I'm afraid we are going to have to do some radical surgery on David's hands," he said.

"What do you mean by radical?" I asked, totally unprepared for the news that followed.

"I mean we're going to have to cut off Davie's fingers."

"No," I said, my pulse rising and my voice beginning to screech a bit.

"I'm afraid we have no other options," he answered firmly.

"All his fingers?" I asked incredulously. "You're going to have to cut off all of Davie's fingers?"

"Portions of them all, yes. There will be enough left to fashion some thumbs and forefingers eventually. We'll just have to cut until the gangrene is gone."

"Gangrene?" I asked, my heart racing.

"That's right, Marie," he said. "Unless we cut his fingers, he will probably loose his hands and possibly his life."

"There must be another option," I argued, pacing up and down the room, feeling myself close to hysteria. "I will see another specialist," I threatened.

"You have that right, Marie," Dr. Achauer answered, "but I already have six different opinions that concur with mine. We shouldn't waste time looking for more."

"Time?" I screeched at him. "You're talking about my son's fingers. We'll take all the time we need. I'll take him to New York. There must be a hospital somewhere that can save his hands. A doctor who does hands only. A place where. . . ."

I began to cry. Dr. Achauer gets upset when patients cry. He left the room. I slumped into the chair and began to scream into my cupped hands. I was screaming for David. I was screaming for myself. I was angry and fearful and terribly alone.

Geri Chambers hurried into the waiting room. She knelt down in front of me and placed her hands on my knees. She stared up at me smiling, waiting patiently for my tears to stop.

"It's all right to cry, Marie," she said at last. "Don't let Dr. Achauer scare the tears out of you," she said.

Between sobs, I asked questions. They were nasty questions about Achauer's competence and the competence of the nursing staff and of the hospital. I asked her about other doctors, other hospitals, other options.

She never interrupted my barrage of insulting questions. She answered those she could and simply nodded sympathetically when there was no easy answer.

"Then he has to lose them," I finally admitted to myself.

"Yes, Marie," she answered, her voice full of understanding. "But, Dr. Achauer will save all he can. And Bob and the nursing team will work to help Davie use what's left of his hands to the best possible advantage. You'll be amazed at what we can do."

That night at Ken and Judy's we cried and prayed and rehashed the options over and over again. Then we gave Davie and his future back into God's care. "How much should this child suffer?" I asked myself again and again. "How much can he take?" He had been on the verge of death for several weeks. He had high fevers most of the time. His blood pressure was low. His heartbeat was extraordinarily fast. Sometimes his heart beat more than two hundred times a minute. I could hear it beating. I could see his chest pumping up and down. I thought his little heart would burst open from its rapid, erratic pace. And I did not know how much longer my heart would last if I had to watch him suffer more.

The next morning, my sister Sandra, who had flown from New York to visit David, and I were waiting for my son to be wheeled past us from surgery to his room in isolation. Dr. Achauer had already informed us that the fingers had been removed successfully. But his words of encouragement did not prepare us for what we saw being wheeled toward us in the hall that day.

David was still unconscious as they pushed him on his bed up the hallway toward his room. His arms were strapped to metal braces holding his hands rigidly in the air above his body. Pins anchored his hands to the braces. There seemed to be nothing left of his fingers but bloody stubs. Pins had been forced through the base of each finger to hold the stump in place. Mesh bandages were wrapped around the portions of each finger that remained. His hands were still dripping blood. I thought of Jesus on the cross.

When I saw David that day, the strength drained out of me. I leaned up against a wall. I thought for sure I would faint. Sandra guided me toward David's room. We had masked and gowned in preparation for his return; we followed the orderlies and a nurse into David's room. I gripped his bed tightly. David lay there with his arms bent at the elbows. His forearms stuck straight up toward the ceiling. The bloody stumps pinned to the braces were only inches from David's eyes. Soon he would awaken. Soon he would open his eyes to a nightmare.

"Can't you at least cover his hands?" I cried at a nurse.

"I'm sorry, Marie. They need to be open to the air," she answered.

At that moment, Dr. Achauer returned. Immediately, I attacked him.

"Excuse, me, Dr. Achauer," I said angrily, "but can't we cover up David's hands before he wakes up and sees them like that?"

I thought how I would feel if I woke up to such a sight. I was constantly amazed at how little thought doctors gave to the feelings of the patients.

"You know," he said to me, "You're right. Perhaps we could devise something."

Later I learned that Dr. Achauer was very sensitive to the feelings of patients, and their families. But he was just too busy getting the patient back to physical health to spend much time caring for the emotional and spiritual needs of a patient. I wish there were more doctors who were sensitive to what the patient and his family are going through. That is why I stayed in that hospital morning, noon, and night. If doctors and nurses could not be alert to the patient's other needs, the patient's mother could.

I usually stayed at the hospital from 8:00 A.M. until 10:00 P.M. I tried to leave after Davie was asleep. He was still drowsy after surgery from the anesthesia, so I left early the evening his fingers were removed.

I loved driving through the gate at Ken and Judy's home in Fullerton. Often I could hear Greg playing the piano in the living room, while in the kitchen Judy and Melanie would be talking over the day's events. Everything would stop when I arrived. The family would gather to hear the day's report. We would laugh or cry, depending on Davie's progress that day. We would have tea. And we would pray.

Every night the family would gather for a reading of the Scriptures and a time of prayer. I cannot tell you what it meant for me to even temporarily be in a family that gathered in their living room at night to read the Bible and pray. It was not a forced routine for the Curtises. They had suffered together. They had survived their own tragic burn. They had cheated death, as David was cheating it, day by day; and they were glad and grateful for the time God had given them together.

Every night, as part of my routine in the Curtis family, I would open the mail that had come for Davie and for me that day from around the world. The day of David's surgery there was another card from The Happy Rabbit, the anonymous letter postmarked City of Industry, California, who wrote David a creative hopeful message almost every day. There was a note from a seven-year-old boy wishing Davie well. There were dozens of cards and letters, and many checks from well-wishers all over the country.

"Oh, a package came for you," Judy interrupted, walking up the stairs in her robe and slippers. We never knew what to expect when a package arrived. I pulled off the tape, tore open the paper, and discovered a colorful bag. Inside the bag was a complete set of Bert and Ernie finger puppets. For a moment I stared in shock at those little felt faces. I put a puppet on each finger and held them up into the light. I wiggled them and made them dance. I began to laugh.

One by one the Curtises gathered to check up on me. I tossed the finger puppets to them and like me, they stared for a moment, thinking of the irony of this gift from a stranger who sent finger puppets, never dreaming they would arrive the day my son's fingers were removed. They, too, began to laugh.

One day when Davie reads this I hope he understands. We had cried the entire day and throughout the awful night before the radical surgery on his hands. We had prayed and hoped that something could be done to save them. Then when he was wheeled into that room with his bloody little stumps reaching out to us, the tears began again. That night the tears were over and laughter filled the room. Sometimes, Davie, laughter is a kind of crying when grieving has left you exhausted and your tears are spent. We just stood in the hallway holding each other and laughing with the finger puppets at our feet. We felt too bad to risk our tears again.

One night before a particularly dangerous surgery, David was afraid for me to leave the hospital. I decided to spend the night on a chair in his room. He had been close to death so many times. He was only six years old. He had survived an attempted murder by his own father. He needed to feel secure. He needed someone to be with him whom he knew and trusted. He needed to feel my presence through the night in that darkened room. Even if he awakened only once, I wanted to be present to reassure him. I wanted to be there to show him that I loved him and that I would not leave him.

"Mrs. Rothenberg?" a resident opened the door to Davie's room and found me on my all-night vigil. "I'm sorry, but you cannot spend the night here."

"Why not?" I asked, whispering so that Davie would not hear. "I'm paying for this room. I can stay in it if I like."

"But the rules, Mrs. Rothenberg," he insisted. "The rules are clear."

"I don't care about your rules," I whispered rather loudly at him. "I care about my son." David had been crying softly before the resident entered.

"Don't leave, Mommy," he cried even louder. "Don't leave me, please."

"Don't worry, David," I comforted him. "I'll be right here. I'm just going outside a minute to talk to this young man. I'll be right back." Talking slowly, calmly, I smiled at my son and inched toward the open door. The minute the door closed between us, I turned on the resident.

"What right do you have, asking me to leave my son's room in the middle of the night when he's terrified? What rule is more important than a six-year-old child's right to have his mother there when he's afraid?"

"You can't just break the rules," he answered. "You aren't running this hospital. Who do you think you are?"

"I'll tell you who I am," I said, pointing my finger at him. "I'm David Rothenberg's mother. David is my son. He's close to death and nobody, not you, not the doctors, not the president, will chase me away." I stared at him while he backed off down the hallway.

"I'll report this," he whispered.

"Tell the world," I whispered back. "Just don't bother us again to-night."

I wasn't nice. Sometimes I overreacted. Other times I let them push me around. But most of the time I stayed in fighting. I believe that in the long run, family members will do almost as much to save patients' lives as the doctors and nurses who treat them. A surgeon's knife, a nurse's syringe, an orderly's chart, or therapist's splints can do so much; but without the constant presence of loving friends or family, the patient may not survive anyway. Having someone there who knows the patient intimately and cares about him and him alone is a guarantee that the patient will not be forgotten or his condition go un-noticed.

There are times a loved one can be more accurate than a doctor or nurse in diagnosing a patient's condition. Just the day before Easter, for example, I began to worry that David was going to die. I even dreamed it. I sat in Davie's room staring at him, knowing that something was wrong. He was lethargic. He was having some difficulty breathing. I rang for a nurse.

"Something's wrong with Davie," I told her when she entered the room.

At first, the nurses at UCI thought I was some kind of crank. Then they began to respect my amateur diagnosis of David's condition. This time they listened.

"What do you think is wrong?" the night nurse asked.

"I don't know what it is," I answered. "That's your job. You have all the equipment and the know-how. I'm just his mother. But I'm sure that something is wrong."

She took his temperature. It was normal. She checked his heartbeat and blood pressure. They were normal as well. She asked him if he was in pain. He said no.

I felt stupid, but still I knew something was not right!

"There's nothing wrong that I can tell," the nurse said after examining David carefully. "Keep watching and report anything that bothers you," she said.

All night long I watched and worried. The next day I continued my complaint. A lung specialist was sent by to check on David's condition. I told him the symptoms I had noticed through the night.

The doctor leaned over David and listened carefully to his lungs.

"Your boy has pneumonia," he said, walking quickly toward the door. "I'll be right back."

107

They suctioned out liters of liquid that were congesting David's lungs. The nurses were amazed at how much fluid had welled up inside him from the pneumonia no one had diagnosed. Almost immediately, David returned to normal. He sat up in bed again. He talked to me again. What would have happened if I had not insisted something was wrong? Would the lung doctor have been sent for? Would anybody have noticed?

That awful day when David saw his amputated fingers for the first time was one more example of how important it is for a friend or member of the family to be standing by.

"Look, Mommy," he said, holding up the bandaged stumps of fingers. "I hurt myself."

What do you say to a child who suddenly notices his fingers have been cut off? What do you tell him when he asks you why? There were no doctors or nurses present. David had been shocked by his discovery. He needed someone just to reassure him that everything was okay.

"You have boo-boos, Davie," I explained. "But they will heal and get better. Don't worry."

Even an unscientific, almost ridiculous answer like that one was better than the silence a patient receives when there is no one in the room to ask.

David came through the next grafting surgery with no apparent problems. Dr. Achauer removed flesh from his left side to graft large portions of his legs, his upper arms, his torso, and portions of his face. Dr. Achauer, Dr. Sankary, and the other members of the UCI Burn Center team were putting my son back together again. Two weeks after Easter, the pins were removed from his fingers. The staples holding the cadaver skin in place were taken out. I relaxed, hoping that the worst was behind us. It was not.

"Mrs. Rothenberg, we have bad news for you." Dr. Achauer had just introduced me to an infectious-disease specialist who had been examining David. John, who had returned to California on one of his regular visits, squeezed my hand as I followed the doctors into the hallway.

"Your son has contracted an infection called candida," he said.

"How serious is it?" I asked, thinking it to be one more infection in a long list of infections David had contracted and conquered. The doctors looked back and forth at each other.

Finally one doctor had the courage to say it straight. "It is usually fatal, I'm afraid."

I sat up in my chair, no longer relaxed, no longer hoping the worst was behind us. "How do you treat it?" I asked.

"Well, we have an antibiotic that may work," the doctor explained, "but it is as poisonous as the bacteria it attacks."

"Are you telling me that after all of this, my son will die?" I asked.

"We don't know," they answered, and then just stood staring at me.

"You don't know?" I asked. "What *do* you know about it?"

"We know David's chances to survive are fifty-fifty. And we know the antibiotic is possibly as toxic to both his kidneys and his liver as the candida is."

"What do you want from me?" I asked, exhausted by the news.

"You have to give us permission to treat the candida, Mrs. Rothenberg," the doctor said, holding out a permission form.

"How can I know what to do?" I questioned. "You're the doctors."

"We can only advise you that we think it is best to try," one doctor said sympathetically. "You have to decide if our diagnosis is correct."

"What can I say?"

Davie's life was threatened again. He had been through four major grafting surgeries already. He had been treated for more infections than I could remember. He had conquered them all. Still, another enemy appeared to threaten him.

"Treat him," I said, taking the paper and signing it as they watched. "Fifty-fifty is better than no chance at all."

I walked away from them toward the waiting room where John and Terry Branum were waiting for me.

"David's going to die," I said, expecting both of them to share my fear and comfort me.

"No, he's not," Terry laughed.

I was stunned. What kind of sympathy was that? David had a fatal infection. I was crying and two of my closest allies were standing there laughing at me.

"David's a fighter," Terry said. "He'll beat this one like he has beaten all the others."

"This is a piece of cake for David," John said. "You know he's a survivor. Quit worrying."

"You watch, Marie, he'll fly right through this one, too," Terry said.

I was angry that they did not hold me and comfort me, but their faith in David turned out to be faith well placed.

The doctors began to administer large doses of the potentially deadly antibiotic to combat the candida in David's system. For a week I watched his body try to fight off the infection. He moved restlessly in his bed, sobbing softly. Even in his sleep, he whimpered. Apparently he felt great pain. I was afraid that any moment he would die.

On the seventh day, I came to the hospital early expecting the worst. Nurses were hurrying in and out of David's room. Dr. Zuckerman rushed down the hall toward me.

"What's wrong with Davie?" I asked, hurrying toward him, trying to tie on my sterile gown and mask.

"His blood pressure has dropped very low, Marie," the doctor informed me. "We're working to keep it from dropping any lower."

"You're going to be okay, David," I said, rushing to his bedside. But I could tell this fight might be his last. He was only half-conscious. His system had been poisoned by the drug designed to save him. They had warned me. Everyone feared that David would go into a coma and not recover. His kidneys had stopped working. There was no urine output whatsoever. Doctors rushed other medicines into him to get his kidneys working and his fluids flowing again. They worked to get his blood pressure up. All morning he teetered back and forth between consciousness and death. Then he smiled wanly.

"We've stabilized him for now," Dr. Zuckerman said. "We'll watch him carefully through the day and hope for the best."

We got the best that day in a kind of medicine no one could prescribe.

Sue Martinez rushed into the room late that day and motioned me to follow her into the hallway. "Guess what?" she said, excited as a teenager. "Reggie Jackson is coming to visit David."

"You're kidding," I said, my own latent adolescence coming to a boil. "How do you know?"

"His manager, Buzzi Bavasi, called and said Reggie would drop by."

I could hardly focus on Sue's account, knowing how important that visit might be to David. When Reggie played for the New York Yankees, my five-year-old son, his father, and I would gather around the television and cheer. We would wait for Reggie to field a hot grounder or take his place at bat. When his home run saved the game, little David would jump up and down shouting, "Reggie, Reggie, Reggie!" If David had one last request, it would be to see Reggie Jackson in the flesh. Come to think of it, it might have been my last request as well.

"Are you sure, Sue?" I asked her, fearing the rumor was too good and too well timed to be true.

"Yes, I am sure," she said, hurrying down the hall. "But don't tell anyone," she whispered over her shoulder loudly as she ran. "We promised we would not tell the press."

Reggie did not want publicity. He wanted to see David. He was going to just drop by. He did not want anyone to know he was coming. He had heard that Davie was a fan and he wanted this fan to know he cared.

"David," I said. David was still weak from his fight with the poisons in his system. He lay staring up at me, half-asleep.

"David, Reggie is coming to visit."

His eyes opened wide. The doctors had hoped for something to get my son out of his slump. It was immediately obvious that Reggie Jackson was just the medicine we needed.

During the afternoon the nurses were a wreck. Everybody, including me, was primping and preparing for the "surprise" visit. Davie lay in the midst of us, his adrenaline beginning to flow in his little body as Reggie's arrival time approached. David had baseball facts for everybody. He reminded us of Reggie's batting average. He wanted Reggie's number up on his bulletin board near his bed. In the midst of the preparation, David whispered to me.

"Mommy, don't let Reggie see my fingers."

I looked at my son. He was one solid scar from head to foot. His hair was gone. He had no ears and only a piece of nose. His lips were burned away. But he did not want Reggie to see his fingers. I had to stand in the hallway for a moment, after that one, choking back my tears and wondering what Reggie would do when he did see David. Then I worried that Reggie might not show up at all. What a terrible blow that would have been to David. It might have been fatal to get his hopes so high and then to take them all away again.

I did not need to worry. Terry Branum walked toward Davie's room with Reggie Jackson in tow. Reggie is a tall, beautiful man. He was wearing white pants and a silk white shirt. He moved so gracefully. It was no wonder nurses up and down the hall were feeling faint.

"Davie, he's coming," I said, rushing into the room.

Then the door pushed open one more time and Reggie Jackson stood looking down at David. He slowly walked toward the bed, the first shock waves reflected in his face. Davie was not easy to look at in those days. Reggie did not speak. He just stood there staring. Davie looked up at Reggie and for a moment he did not speak, either. The room was silent. David spoke first.

"How's your hamstring, Reggie?" he asked.

The irony of that question will live in my heart forever. My son was fighting for his life against a near-fatal infection. He was still facing serious grafting and amputation surgeries. Gangrene was growing in his

111

back where the grafting still waited to be done, but he was thinking about Reggie and the hamstring muscle that endangered Reggie's game.

For a very brief moment Reggie looked stunned. Then he moved to David's side.

"It's fine, David," he answered. "Thanks for asking. But what about you? How are you doing?"

"I'm okay," Davie said. "Are you going to play tomorrow?"

They talked baseball that day and it was perhaps the best antitoxic medicine my son could receive. Reggie gave Davie a child-size Angels uniform with the number 44 on the front and David's name printed on the back, an Angels hat, and an autographed baseball that read, "To my special friend, David."

"I'll be back, David," Reggie promised. I could see that a national hero and his number-one fan were both having trouble blinking back their tears.

"Who's the mother?" Reggie asked, leaning quickly up from David and walking toward me. Together we walked to the door. "See you Friday," he said over his shoulder to my son.

Then we were outside the room. Reggie paused. He placed one hand over his eyes and repeated to himself, "How's your hamstring, Reggie?" Almost in tears, he said, "The kid's practically dead and he's asking me about my hamstring?"

Then Reggie looked me squarely in the eye. "If there is anything I can do for that boy, you just let me know."

"You've already done so much," I said. "Thanks for coming." Then I began to cry. He looked awkward and helpless. I smiled at him and went back to David's side.

Already the visit was making a difference. David was nearly beside himself with excitement. Geri Chambers placed the tiny uniform in his arms.

"Will it fit me, Mommy?" he asked.

"Someday, David," I answered. "Someday soon."

He hugged the uniform in his arms, the stubs of his fingers finally outside the covers where he had hidden them.

"Wasn't he nice, Mommy?" David said, cradling the uniform in his arms, new life flowing through his body.

"Yes, David. He was nice, so very nice to come."

10

Two days after Reggie Jackson's first visit, the Buena Park Police Department sponsored a Crime Prevention Fair to promote safety and good health in the city. There would be autograph booths featuring celebrities who were donating that day to charities sponsored by the police. Burt Bacharach, the music composer and conductor, and the popular singing star Roberta Flack were featured guests. They were going to donate and autograph records to be sold to help pay David's bills.

The Buena Park Police Department had established a fund on David's behalf. All the money that was sent in the various cards and letters we received was deposited in that fund administered by Terry Branum and the Buena Park police. David's hospital bills were accumulating in the tens of thousands of dollars. The Buena Park Police Wives sponsored a bake sale in a local shopping mall. They raised three thousand dollars for David's fund. Every night I opened cards and letters with gifts as small as twenty-five cents from a child's bank to five thousand dollars from a corporation. Burt Bacharach had already written a check for one thousand dollars for the fund. I was looking forward to meeting both him and Roberta Flack. I wanted to thank them for their kindness to David. But at the hospital that morning my plans were suddenly changed.

I had taken an extra cup of coffee in the hospital cafeteria. I felt relaxed and excited at the same time. Since Reggie's visit, David seemed to improve steadily. There were signs that the potentially fatal candida infection was being conquered by the dangerous but effective antibiotic. David's spirits were high. Soon his badly burned back would be grafted. He had survived the other surgeries and seemed to be mending steadily. The grafts were taking hold. Only one last major area needed to be covered. I was counting the days until David would be taken off the critical list.

Usually, the nurses spent longer on David's bath than they planned. They worked hard on him to be sure his grafts were holding and that the infections were being knocked down. I wandered up to the intensive-care unit looking forward to my hour-long break with Burt Bacharach and Roberta Flack later that day.

Then I noticed that something was wrong in David's room. I could feel the panic a hundred yards away. Nurses were scurrying about. Doctors were trying to get a respirator tube down his throat.

"What's wrong?" I gasped.

Geri Chambers, the charge nurse, hurried over to me. She looked scared. Like the other nurses at UCI, Geri Chambers is normally a calm, caring, hardworking professional. She wasn't calm that day.

"We have a problem, Marie," she said. "Something happened to David in the bath."

"What happened?" I blurted out, looking at the doctors still trying to force the tube down Davie's throat.

"We don't know. As he came out of the bath, he started having trouble breathing. His throat closed up. He began turning blue."

"Oh, God," I said. "What are they doing to my baby?"

"They're trying to intubate him again, Marie," she said. "They must get that tube down through his throat so that he can breathe again."

Emergency signals were sounding through the hospital. An anesthesiologist rushed in with his equipment. Dr. Sankary arrived on the scene, followed by various specialists, all working to save David. Whatever they tried, they could not intubate him. The tube just wouldn't go through the swollen throat. David's room looked like an operating room.

Dr. Howard Sankary, normally a man of unusual calm, approached me.

"We don't know what to do, Marie," he confessed. "We're trying another procedure on him now. The tube must be placed. If this one doesn't work, there's just nothing else we can do."

"What happened?" I asked angrily. "What caused his throat to constrict again?"

"We don't know why it closed and we don't really know what to do about it. But we are doing our best. Excuse me."

I knew then why doctors may feel the need to lie. It is bad enough that they have to face alone the mystery and sometimes treachery of the human body; but to face it with the patient's family knowing the doctor's limits must be doubly difficult.

Kitty, a favorite nurse of David, came running from the room. She was crying.

"I'm sorry, Marie," she confessed. "I'm not supposed to say this, but it is up to God now. They can't get that thing in. Pray. If David lives, it will be a miracle."

"Lord, help David," I prayed. "I don't want to lose him now."

Inside the room, a specialist removed a syringe and pushed the needle deep into David's neck. The drug paralyzed him temporarily and this time the tube slipped through the constriction. The respirator flashed on. Oxygen flowed freely into David's lungs. He began to breathe more easily again. The blue-tinged skin returned to pink. I rushed to a telephone.

"Officer Branum, please," I told the police dispatcher.

"Terry? This is Marie. The doctors are having trouble with David. He can't breathe. His throat is blocked. They got the tube in but they just don't know what will happen next."

"I'm sorry, Marie," Terry said. "I'll be right down."

"No," I told him. "Don't come. I know how long you've been working on the Crime Prevention Fair. You're needed there. But please tell Burt Bacharach and Roberta Flack that I just can't leave Davie until I know he's going to be okay."

"I'll call them, Marie," he said.

"Apologize for me, will you?"

I called Ken and Judy next. Judy came immediately to the hospital. Ken joined Terry at the fair to meet people who had prepared gifts for David. Then they both came to the hospital and joined us at David's bedside.

We stood there, the four of us, watching one more time as David struggled for his life. I don't know what I would have done without those three special people. Terry had represented the Buena Park Police Department from the beginning. He had begun the fund to help pay David's bills. He had represented us to the press and to the public. And Ken and Judy and their family had been my link with God during those most terrifying times. I don't remember a day that either Ken or Judy or both didn't come to the hospital. I don't remember a night they weren't waiting to comfort me after another tragic or routine hospital day. Now they stood beside me once again watching David, praying for his survival, and giving me strength and hope by their presence.

David's fever was high those next few days. The candida infection was kicking up again. The swelling in his throat continued. It was a bad time. David was discouraged. I was tired out. I sat there watching David suffer, feeling helpless and angry and frustrated. I wondered what awful thing would happen to him next. No one noticed the door to Davie's room open quietly.

"May I come in?" someone asked.

"Reggie," David gasped from the bed, seeing his hero Reggie Jackson standing in the doorway.

I jumped up and went to the door. This time Reggie carried an armload of baseball artifacts—so many, in fact, that we auctioned some of them off at the Crime Prevention Fair for Davie's fund.

"I hear you're not having a fun day," Reggie said, walking over to David.

"I'm thirsty, Mommy," David moaned. The words were almost indecipherable, but I could understand them. "I'm thirsty," he said over and over again. "I'm thirsty." Reggie Jackson and I stood there helpless. David's body was red with fever.

"Please give him something to drink," Reggie whispered to Geri as she took David's vital signs.

"We can't, Mr. Jackson," she said, "when he's on the respirator. We're afraid anything he drinks might go into his lungs and create more problems."

"Can't he have *something?*" Reggie asked again.

"Well, maybe," she said, writing David's pulse rate on his chart and walking from the room.

She returned a few moments later.

"He can have a sip of water every five minutes," she informed us, "but nothing more, I'm afraid."

Immediately Reggie reached for the water glass and bent down over my son.

"Come on, slugger," he said. "Just a sip, now."

David quit moaning. He took a quick drink from the cup in his hero's hand.

"How's that?" Davie's wonderful new nurse asked him.

"Good," Davie answered, smiling weakly. "Good," he said again.

Every five minutes for almost an hour, Reggie Jackson gave a sip of water to my son. He kept track of those passing minutes with the accuracy of a trained athlete.

"Five minutes," he would say on the second, and David would smile and drink again.

Davie was six years old. His body was riddled with infection. His back was gangrenous. He was fighting for survival, and again, an unexpected visit from his new friend made all the difference.

"How are you doing?" Reggie asked me when finally he had to leave.

"I'm doing much better now, thank you," I answered. Then he turned and walked away from us down the hospital corridor.

"Is he here?" A nurse rushed into the room just as Reggie disappeared down the hallway. Then another nurse and another appeared until the room was filled. They all bragged about David and his new friendship with Reggie. Again, with just a quick hello, Reggie Jackson brought strength to my son and hope to all of us. I know what it cost him in time and extra planning to visit David half a dozen times in those months, but the results paid one hundred times in the life of a little boy to whom those visits made a fantastic difference.

But the problem had not ended. Later that day, Dr. Achauer hurried into the room. He read David's chart, then rolled him slowly onto his stomach. I gasped. David's back had been the part of his body burned most seriously. Apparently he fell onto the blazing synthetic rug in his motel room that night. The hot, melting carpet had fused onto his back. The burn was deep and very serious. The area was pussy with gangrene.

"We have to graft him right away," Dr. Achauer explained. "The back is twenty percent of his body. The other grafts are holding now. We just can't wait longer. We must try to help him fight that infection and prevent other infections from occurring." Judy, Ken, and I stared at David's little back. It was truly the worst thing I had seen during our stay in the Burn Ward. It looked like a burned pizza. There was no better way to describe it. His back was a mass of burned, bloody, broken flesh. It was full of infection. The color ranged from black through the spectrum of white, green, and pink tissue. How Dr. Achauer could

117

graft that wide area with such a thin net of David's skin was beyond comprehension.

The very next day, David was taken into the operating room for the major graft surgery. Another small patch of healthy skin one-one hundredth of an inch thick was shaved from his donor site. The skin was perforated. The net of tissue was formed, then grafted over David's back and a large portion of his right arm where grafts had not yet taken hold.

David lost five pints of blood during that surgery. As we waited the next four days, the vascular system beneath David's skin joined with the blood vessels in that microscopically thin layer of grafted tissue. Blood began to flow in David's back again. Skin grew out to meet skin. Scars were formed where the two epidermal layers met and joined. The infection was stopped. The back began to heal. David was sitting up and joking with Ken and Judy and me in his room.

"How does it look?" I asked Dr. Achauer, praying desperately that the graft had taken hold.

"Look for yourself," he said proudly.

We crowded around David's bare back. The awful bloody pizza was gone. David's skin covered his back in a network of red scars and new pink tissue.

"David," Ken said, "you and God did it again."

David laughed his gruff, embarrassed laugh. "Doesn't look like a pizza anymore, eh?"

We were surprised. He had heard us. How often he lay there as though asleep, hearing everything we had said. How foolish it made us feel. Nurses came in to prepare David for his bath. Orderlies wheeled him toward the hydro room.

"We will know a lot more about this graft after Davie's bath," Dr. Achauer explained to us. "But generally, I can tell you we are out of the woods."

I looked at him skeptically. How many times before I had thought David was "out of the woods," and every time I had been disappointed. But Dr. Achauer seemed so certain.

"Getting his body grafted," Dr. Achauer went on, "means he's no longer acute. The hospital spokesman will tell the press today that David's condition has been upgraded from critical to serious. There are still dangers, but we are through the woods."

Actually, there were terrible surprises ahead, but this victory seemed worth celebrating.

"We have saved his life," Achauer said. "Now we can get on with the rehabilitation tasks."

"While we were grafting," he explained, "we just held our breath. We didn't know if David had enough living skin to replace the burned, dead skin. We just kept cutting off the old and replacing with new, hoping the grafts would hold and cover. They have."

Dr. Achauer left us to inspect Davie's grafts more carefully. When he returned, he was smiling even more broadly.

"David's back looks wonderful!" he exclaimed. "At first we were nervous," he confessed, "because some of the grafts didn't look like they were taking shape around the edges. But we finally got a good look and everything has taken just spectacularly."

"Let me see your scars, Kenny," David said, as he had said so many times. And once again, Ken stood before my son. He turned slowly so that David could see how well his friend's burns had healed.

"How long before my skin looks like Kenny's?" David asked Dr. Achauer.

Ken's scars were beautiful by anyone's standards. His arms and legs, neck and back had been totally engulfed in flames. The grafting had taken several months. In less than a year, it was already difficult to tell that his skin had been almost totally replaced.

"You will look better and better as the days go by," Dr. Achauer answered.

David was out of danger, or so we thought. With most of his body grafted, the problems of infection had been eliminated.

David didn't speak. He looked at the doctor, then at Ken, then back to the doctor once again. Finally he spoke.

"When I get my new face," David whispered, "I want it to look like Kenny's."

We were stunned. I moved to David's side and grasped his hand. Ken and Judy moved in closer to David's bed. Dr. Achauer walked quickly from the room. Only days before, David had asked to see his burned face for the first time. I couldn't refuse. He took a small compact mirror and stared for the longest time. Then he lay back on his pillow, lost in thought. Now I knew what he had been thinking.

Of course, if was impossible to duplicate Ken's face on David, but I believe even David knew he was saying far more than that. Ken had been in that hospital room almost every day. David insisted on seeing Ken's scars over and over again. They were smooth and pink and beautiful. It reassured my son to think that one day he, too, would have skin like that.

11

At last David was taken off the critical list. We both felt such relief after the nonstop pressure of the past three months. Hospital visits seemed more routine. I didn't walk into the Burn Center expecting Davie's room to look like a disaster area. I didn't grow clammy every time the telephone rang at Ken and Judy's home. I had time to reflect on the past eleven weeks, and how we had survived them.

As I looked back, I realized how crucial Ken and Judy Curtis had been to both David and me during those first three months. Every time David faced a crisis, I would call Judy or Ken. The conversations were almost always the same.

"Judy," I would say, "David is having a very bad day."

"I'm sorry, Marie," she would answer. "Tell me what's happening."

"I think he's going to die," I would say, usually crying. "Could you start praying for him?"

"Okay, honey," Judy would always promise. "I've been praying all day. But I'll call in the troops."

Then Judy would call her church and tell them the latest news about David. Church secretaries would call members of Judy's Bible-study group. They would call their friends and families. In just a matter of minutes, dozens of people were mobilized to pray for David. I didn't know how much good those prayers would do. I just knew I had no other option. When the doctors were unsure what to do next, all we could do was pray. And I felt so much better when I knew Judy's friends were praying.

Once the prayer people had been notified, Judy and/or Ken would immediately drive to the hospital to be with me. There were many times when we would just sit in the waiting room watching the clock, waiting for the doctors or the nurses to complete their medical procedures.

"Marie," Judy or Ken would say during those awful times of waiting, "you've got to leave it up to God now."

I would nod, knowing it was all they could say. At first it made me angry. I wanted to do something for David myself. But I was helpless. I had to leave it up to God. They were right. I didn't like that uncomfortable, helpless feeling. I wanted to produce a miracle, but I couldn't.

"What's going to happen will happen," Judy said over and over again. "But since God loves David, whatever happens will be for his good."

Then we would pray. We would grab hands. We would bow our heads and Ken or Judy would begin their quiet conversation with God.

"Lord, be with Marie today," they would pray. "Father, give Marie and Davie strength to get through this new problem. . . ."

I couldn't pray then as they prayed. I didn't know what to say or how to say it. I felt embarrassed when I tried. I was used to repeating "Our Father" or "Hail Mary" or reading a prayer to Saint Jude or Saint Paul, but when Ken and Judy prayed they talked directly to our Father. It was beautiful. It left me confused and, at the same time, at peace.

Then they would wait with me until Davie's crisis had been resolved. They were my constant assurance that everything was going to be all right. They were always at my side. Only a few months before, Ken and Judy had been strangers. Now they were more than friends. They were my new family, and I was constantly surprised by their love and their faithfulness.

I sat in David's room that day remembering all they had done for me. They gave me a place in their home. They came regularly to see my son in the hospital. They listened to my problems every day for three months. They never complained. They never asked, "What are you going to do for us?" They never made me feel like a burden. They never showed resentment. They never asked me for payment.

A night nurse caught me lost in thought. "Don't you feel it's time to go home, Marie?"

I must have looked half asleep as I sat thinking in the chair beside David's bed.

"David is sleeping now," she said. "And he's off the critical list. Why don't you go home and get some rest before we have to put *you* on it?"

I looked at my watch. It was past 11:00 P.M. I suppose it was difficult to really believe that Davie was through the worst of it. There was no use waiting around for another crisis to develop.

"Good night, Davie," I said to my sleeping son. Then I looked down at him. Splints held his arms out from his body at right angles. Splints held his little hands firmly in place. A neck collar forced his head back rigidly. Another night splint was screwed into his mouth. He had gauze and ointment covering his entire body. Blood from the still-healing grafts had soaked through everything. I knew the days ahead would be long and exhausting. I wondered how he would get through them. I wondered how I would survive.

Driving out of the UCI Medical Center parking lot and up State College Boulevard to Judy and Ken's, I remembered how often they had told me it was their Christian community—Jesus and His people—who had gotten them through Ken's burns and their own long, exhausting days of grafting and healing. I had been attending their church for several weeks.

Worship at the Eastside Christian Church was so different from the Sunday masses of my childhood. Before the service, families gathered in the lobby of the church, on the steps, and in the parking lot. They seemed sincerely glad to be together. They shook hands and hugged. They talked about God and what God had been doing in their lives as freely as they talked about the weather or the baseball scores. Inside the rock-and-wood sanctuary they shared brown hymnbooks and sang simple gospel songs and hymns with a kind of enthusiasm I had never experienced. The words of the sermon were helpful and easy to understand.

Every Sunday, during the pastoral prayer, the minister, Ben Merold, would report on David's condition. When he finished telling of David's current struggle in the intensive-care unit, the people would groan audibly in sympathy and concern. Then someone would pray for Davie and the whole congregation would "amen" quietly as one. As they prayed their loving prayers, I pictured my son lying on his hospital bed. I could imagine Jesus hearing their prayers, walking up to my son's bed, and touching him. Doctors and nurses would be hurrying in and out of the room. They couldn't see the Stranger standing there, but I could, and these dear praying people could. The doctors couldn't know that He was there, in the room with Davie, watching over him, making him well. But I knew it was true and His people knew it was true. How could I doubt, even if it was the natural thing to do.

I will always be grateful for the important role the dedicated doctors played in my son's recovery. Without their skills, there would have been no healing. But I also saw what happened when people prayed. Doctors would be startled by Davie's "turn for the better." Nurses would be amazed by my son's "unusual progress." But I knew, and God's people knew, who was really responsible for every little miracle along the way. Every time the people would pray for David in those services, I would cry. Judy held me and comforted me. She would say, "The Lord is with him, Marie." She would cry too, but both of us knew she was right. The Lord was with David through the prayers of these people. It was He who healed and saved my son.

At the close of each service, new believers were baptized into the Body of Christ in a rock-framed baptismal pool behind the pulpit. Sunday after Sunday I watched people walk forward to make professions of their faith and then be baptized as the organ played softly and the people prayed.

I drove home from the hospital thinking of Judy and Ken, their church, and the difference they had made in our lives. Judy was waiting for me when I arrived at her home that night. The tea was on as usual. Judy was reading. She looked up when I entered.

"Hi, Marie," she said, standing up and walking toward me with a small, beautifully wrapped box in her hand. "How's Davie?"

"Oh, he's fine," I said glibly, too tired to give an adequate report on what had been another awful but routine day in intensive care.

"Here, I have a little surprise," Judy said, handing me the box.

"Judy, you don't need to give me gifts," I said, protesting again all the loving surprises Judy and Ken had given me along the way.

"Open it," she demanded, grinning.

I pulled off the ribbon and tore the paper away. Inside the box was a gold chain with a beautiful gold moon and a diamond star by its side. I was stunned. It had been one of Judy's own treasures.

"Happy Mother's Day," she said.

I stood there in shock. No matter how hard I blinked I could not stop the tears. Judy held me in her arms as I cried.

"I've never had such a special Mother's Day gift before," I said, embarrassed and grateful. I had done my best to be a good mother to my son, but look where it had gotten him. I cried for Davie lying in that

Burn Center, and I cried for myself. I felt as though I had failed my son. But I was exhausted from trying to come through for him and that Mother's Day gift triggered a landslide of emotions.

"Thank you, Judy," I said, swallowing hard for control. I wanted to tell her so many things. Instead we just stared at each other for a moment. She was crying, too. Finally I turned and walked up the stairs to my bedroom.

Grandma June, Judy's mother, was still up. Her light was on and her door was open.

"Come and visit, Marie," she said as I passed by.

She saw I had been crying. I sat down beside her. Slowly, words came. She, too, had grown up in a Catholic home. We had much in common.

"I don't understand Judy," I said. "She and Ken are so loving. I've been afraid that they were out to get something from me. They aren't."

"They do it all because of Jesus," Grandma June said, as she had said so many times before.

I had never liked the expression "because of Jesus." It was an idea I couldn't grasp. Jesus was so real to this whole family and so distant to me. I pictured Him hanging on a cross with blood dripping from His hands and feet and side. I visualized Him in the pictures from catechism classes looking holy and plastic and distant. I pictured Him in movies wearing a beard, a bathrobe, and sandals, wandering around the desert speaking parables and sounding like a priest.

But to Ken and Judy, Jesus was real. He was alive. They weren't crazy or spooky or other-worldly. I had proven that to myself. They were real. But Jesus was just as real to them as they were real to me. They talked to Him as they talked to me. They read His words from the Bible as though they were written just for them. They talked about Him to me and to their friends as though they had just seen Him at lunch.

"Grandma June, I don't understand it," I said. "How come Jesus is so real to your kids and so unreal to me?"

As we talked that night, our voices carried down the hall into Ken and Judy's room. In pajamas and slippers, they joined us. We sat talking until almost 2:00 A.M. I peppered them with questions that had been piling up in my brain.

"Would your marriage be as good as it is just because of your personalities, or does Jesus really make a difference? You and your family get along so well. Is that because you just happen to be the get-along types, or does Jesus really have anything to do with it? Did you get through your own burns because you are tough eggs, or did Jesus really help you through the ordeal?"

Questions poured out of me. I already knew their answers. I thought maybe if I heard them all again, it would make sense.

"People don't understand the strength that Jesus gives you," Judy began again. "I don't even understand it. When we were in the hospital with Kenny, the burn people watched him in the tub and in the intensive-care unit. He was covered with third-degree burns. He suffered unbelievable pain but Kenny just kept crying, "Sweet Jesus. Sweet Jesus. Be with me. Please help me through the pain."

"I kept thinking of His picture on my wall," Kenny interrupted. "The pain was terrible, but I just pictured Jesus there in the hydro room with me. His eyes followed me wherever I moved. He was always there with me. The worse the pain got, the closer I felt Him."

"An orderly said, 'He's going to crack,' " Judy remembered. " 'Your husband needs to get angry and rebel. What's the matter with him? He needs a psychiatrist.' "

"Judy just smiled at their worries," Ken said, "and held me. When my veins popped and my whole body oozed blood, she just hung on and said over and over, 'Dear Jesus, be with Kenny. Dear Jesus, be with Kenny.' All through those first long weeks of pain, we said His name over and over again and He was there. I don't have to prove it to anyone—that Judy didn't faint or run screaming from the sight of me; that I didn't just give up and die; that we both didn't grow angry and bitter and seek revenge was proof enough for both of us. Those angry, awful emotions are what comes naturally, Marie," he said. "Jesus gave us love and peace instead. He made a terrific difference. You just have to decide about Him yourself. Then you'll see for yourself the difference that He makes."

"But other people get through pain without Him," I protested. "What about them?"

"We only know about us," Ken said. "We only know the difference He has made in our lives."

I looked up into Ken's eyes and then into Judy's and June's. They all wanted me to "trust Jesus." They were hoping I would "accept Him as my Lord and Saviour." But they didn't force me. They certainly never stopped talking about Him, but they never got pushy or offensive. They accepted me. They loved me. They helped me in the worst time of my life and never once complained, but they didn't force the issue. They waited and they loved.

"I want to become a Christian," I said after a long, thoughtful pause. But as they moved to hug me, tears streaming down their faces, I stepped back, raised my arm, and said, "But I can't. I can't go down to the front of the church before all those people. I don't feel sincere doing it in public like that."

"Decide to follow Him when and where you want," Judy said. "Going forward or joining a Christian church are just ways of making public what has already been decided in private."

Again we grabbed hands in prayer. I couldn't pray out loud without running out of words and feeling stupid. But I tried. Ken and Judy and June all prayed for me again. Then, still grasping that Mother's Day gift in my fist, I hurried into my own room and closed the door.

I didn't understand much about Christian faith but I did understand that the Christians in my life had made the difference for me and for my son in a terrible time of tragedy and stress. I stared at the little gold moon and the silver diamond star. And I knew that when the morning sun rose on another Sunday, I could not postpone my decision much longer.

The sermon ended. The pastor, Ben Merold, invited those who would like to make their confession of faith to come forward at that time. I couldn't go up there. I was afraid. Other people moved down the aisles. The ministers laid their hands on the people and prayed. Two young men were baptized. The final hymn was sung. The benediction was prayed. And the church emptied out. As I left the church, I felt as though I had failed Ken and Judy Curtis and all my new Christian friends.

So many times, at the close of a service, Judy or Ken had asked, "Would you like to give yourself to the Lord, Marie?" At first it made me angry. *Why do they want me to do this?* I thought, feeling upset. They weren't pushy. They made no demands, but they never stopped asking. I wanted to please them. But I knew I couldn't decide to become a Christian just to make them happy. That was a serious step. I felt God might even punish me or David if I did something so insincere. It would make a mockery of God.

Still, I had to admit that there were many Sunday mornings when I wanted to walk to the front of the church with all the others. I wanted to stand before the whole congregation and say, "I give myself to God." But I couldn't. I was holding back because everyone knew me.

They had read about David's tragedy in the papers. They had seen me on television. I was afraid they would think I was insincere. I was afraid they would wonder if I was going forward just because I wanted God to help my son.

The people of this church had come through for us. In fact, Christian people from around the country had come to our aid. They sent me cards, letters, and money. It was phenomenal the way they reached out to love us. But I didn't want to be baptized as an act of gratitude. They hadn't helped David and me as a way to "get us into the fold." They said they did it in Christ's name because He had told them to love all people in need. And as I received their kindness, I felt God's love as I had not felt it before. Now, I was about ready to give myself back to Him in gratitude for what He had done for me. I knew that He had forgiven my sins. I knew that He loved me and that He was working to heal my son's badly burned body and my angry, anxious heart.

Still, I told myself over and over, *You have to be sure. You have to know what you're doing.* I couldn't do it for Ken and Judy. I couldn't do it for David. I couldn't do it for the church. I had to do it for me because I was convinced, because I had seen something in Jesus and in His people that I wanted for myself. Sometime during the long Mother's Day conversation and that Sunday-morning service, the doubting back and forth finally took a turn toward faith.

Later that night, after spending the afternoon with David in the hospital, I drove back to Ken and Judy's. I felt ashamed and frustrated that I hadn't followed through on my decision.

"I'd like to be baptized," I told Judy that night, "but I just can't walk up there in front of everybody and do it."

The pastor arranged to meet me later in the week for a private confession of faith and a service of baptism. Thursday I left the hospital early; together Ken, Judy, and I drove into the parking lot of the Eastside Christian Church. I was scared and excited. Judy led me into a dressing room and helped me into a baptismal robe. Then we stood together before the small crowd of friends and family who had gathered. Ken and Judy, Melanie and Greg sat together in the front row. Beside them sat Ken and Peg Schmidt, the young Christian couple who had loaned me their car. Judy's Bible-study group was there in force, all smiling up at me, many with tears in their eyes.

The pastor asked me simple questions.

"Yes, I trust Christ as Saviour and Lord," I answered.

127

"Yes, I know He has forgiven me," I said, with growing feelings of certainty.

"Yes, I will do my best to follow Him the rest of my life," I said, more sure than I had ever been.

Beautiful words were read and spoken that day, but I hardly heard them. Was it all a part of a loving God's master plan? Had He taken this terrible tragedy and turned it into something beautiful by His presence? Had He heard and answered the scared and angry prayers I prayed during that airplane ride across the country and in that Holiday Inn during those lonely nights in California? Was this the first step in a lifelong journey for David and for me?

"Marie," Pastor Merold said, one arm around my back, the other reaching up to bless me, "I baptize you in the name of the Father, the Son, and the Holy Spirit."

Then it was over. "Amen," he said. "Amen," the people answered. In minutes, dozens of loving hands reached out to welcome me into His kingdom. And though I was still battling doubt, though I had no idea where it all might end, I felt Him standing there beside them. I felt His hand reach out to me. And somehow I began to understand the difference He would make for the long and frightening days and nights ahead.

12

The hospital corridors were almost dark. The night nurses were at
their stations filling in reports and talking quietly to each other. No
one noticed me as I passed en route to Davie's room. His entire body
was covered with Silvadene cream and bandages. For a moment, in the
darkness, it looked as though his skin were smooth and white again.
Splints held his arms and legs and neck in place. In spite of everything,
he slept. Above his bed hung the bottle of Traumacal, a high-protein,
high-calorie, high-carbohydrate liquid delivering five thousand calo-
ries of nutrients into his system every day. I had come to say good
night and leaned down to kiss him gently on one masked cheek. Then,
in the semidarkness, I noticed that the monitor charting David's heart
rate was fluctuating erratically. I was afraid he was having cardiac arrest.

Quickly I ran to the nursing station.

"There's something wrong with David's monitor," I said to one of
the nurses. "Please come and check." I ran back to the room, looked
down at his bed, and discovered a pool of blood near his right arm.

I hurried back to the nurse's station. "There's blood all over David's
bed and you had better come in right now!"

While David slept, a faulty catheter had cracked. It was an arterial
line. The blood was spurting out. He could have bled to death lying in
a hospital intensive-care unit. Immediately, the nurses stopped the

bleeding and replaced the faulty catheter. David didn't even awaken. It was one more proof to me of my importance as a mother in that place. From the beginning I had served my son as his one twenty-four-hour nurse. I will be grateful forever for the nurses who watched over David during his long hospital stay, but there is no way a nurse who has a dozen other chores, reports to fill out, doctors to obey, and families to please can take totally adequate care of someone as critically burned as David. In spite of the occasional condescending remarks and arrogant or angry looks, I stayed.

At the beginning, although I respected Dr. Achauer and the staff of the UCI Medical Center Burn Center, I threatened to remove David from the hospital if they would not let me stay with him. Dr. Achauer called a meeting of his staff with me present to consider my demands. They decided that I could stay with David when I wanted, unless my presence actually endangered his progress. There were occasional nasty residents or cranky night nurses who tried to rewrite that policy with an angry demand or a sarcastic jibe but, for the most part, the people at UCI welcomed and appreciated my presence.

I often spoke too loudly and too long on David's behalf. Sometimes I was quick to criticize or question before I understood. I yelled at people whom I knew were doing their very best. I blamed people who were not responsible for various ills, large or small, that came David's way. I erred many times, but I erred on my son's behalf. And it wasn't long before I realized even those I yelled at were cheering for both of us.

Dr. Achauer appointed me in charge of Davie's splints. I had complained about the sloppy way they were often Velcroed into place and how often they slipped down and weren't noticed by an attending nurse. Every day I helped David in and out of those splints. And almost every day my son complained about the way I was treating or mistreating him. It was good to see him halfway normal again.

If I complained that David's bath had been too sloppy, Dr. Achauer gave me the power to demand another bath. If raw, open spots on David's body had not been covered with Silvadene, I could request to have them redressed. It wouldn't be long until I was totally responsible for Davie. If there were no more disasters, I soon would have him home and be responsible for his care. Every moment I spent watching the nurses work with David in the hospital, I was training myself for the day when all the chores would be mine.

The hospital had no training program for parents, spouses, family, or friends. I learned those basic nursing skills on my own. If I hadn't insisted on working with my son every day, I would not have been prepared to help him. By watching closely what he was going through, I learned about his suffering and how to help relieve it.

"No!" David yelled at me one evening when I tried to force his forearm into the new night splint.

"What's wrong with it?" I answered, trying to cram his arm down into the concave tubular brace that kept it from drawing in on itself in the night.

"It hurts, Mommy," was all he could say. "Please don't make me wear it."

Finally, I quit trying to force his arm into the splint and looked closely at it. One look and I knew what the problem was. The brace didn't fit. David had been right. I was trying to get his arm into someone else's brace. Who knows how it happened. It just did. And by listening to his complaints, I discovered the error. It is easy to stop listening to one who is constantly in pain.

Watching David day by day, I learned when he was really hurting and when he was only copping out. That's another reason a parent should stay in the hospital. It was the only way I knew to understand what he was going through. The more I understood his pain, the better I was able to help him face it.

"Okay, David," a night nurse said one evening to my son, "roll over onto this stretcher."

She had pushed a gurney into the room to take David off his bed to change his sheets. She parked the gurney directly alongside David's bed. She asked my son to get from his bed onto that stretcher by himself.

"I can't," he moaned.

One look at him was enough to prove him right. He was immobilized by bandages and splints. His skin grafts were still new. His body was stiff with new scars. He was in pain and the distance between his bed and the gurney seemed an infinity.

"Yes, you can," the nurse said abruptly, hurrying about the room without even looking at him closely.

"No, he can't," I interrupted, standing up and moving to defend him. "Look at him. You want him to climb out of bed onto that rickety thing. You're crazy."

She stopped and looked at me. She didn't look at David. She didn't stop to consider me or reconsider David's painful condition. She put her hands on her hips and said, "Yes, he can; only we're not going to make him, are we?"

It was a sarcastic and insensitive remark. The next day I made a formal complaint. The regular nurses were quick to back me. "Of course he couldn't get across that space," Geri Chambers told me. "No telling what the movement would have done to his new grafts. And he might have fallen," she said, shaking her head. "Don't worry, Marie. You were right. Stick to it."

However, there were occasions during that rehabilitation time when I was wrong. Bob Schneider was David's occupational therapist. The first time he worked on David, I almost threw him bodily from the room.

"Good morning," he said, during the first week David was in the UCI Burn Center. "I'm here to work on David."

Immediately alarms sounded. I stood up and moved slowly toward the bed. At the time David was simply a mass of open, burned flesh. His head was still swollen grotesquely. His eyes were closed. He couldn't speak. The grafting had not yet begun. David was still covered in white Silvadene cream and net bandages. And this young therapist plopped into the room, walked up to my son, and began to unbend David's arms. He groaned in pain and tried to pull away. Bob continued stretching the burned and bloody tissue. David groaned louder. I couldn't stand it.

"Get away from him," I whispered, with all the menace a mad mommy could muster.

"I'm sorry, Mrs. Rothenberg," he said. "I know it's hurting David, but we have no choice."

I had been told before I had no choice. And those telling me soon learned I had plenty of choices. My back arched. I stood up on my full five feet five inches and said one more time, "Get away from him."

"Mrs. Rothenberg," he said, "your son's body will begin to contract upon itself. His hands will claw. His arms will bend in upon themselves. His body will automatically contract into the fetal position. If we don't stop that contracting, he will be forever bent. His arms and legs will be useless. His hands will dangle at his sides."

Later Bob took me to his therapy room. He showed me how splints are made from a malleable white plastic material that you could heat and bend permanently into place. He showed me the different dexterity tools. There was a "bird cage," a large, wooden cell with bars of various shapes and sizes. A patient moved inside and gripped those bars over and over again. I watched a burn patient move slowly into the cage. I watched him pull himself up those long wooden slats, inch by painful inch.

"Good boy, Chung Fu," Bob commended him. "Keep after it."

Another child burn victim was working at a long bench, screwing and unscrewing bolts from the wooden frame before him. Two older patients were playing tic-tac-toe, gripping the markers and moving them with their stubby fingers.

"This is where we measure for the Jobst garments," he told me. "These special elastic suits fit skintight. They keep the scars from knotting up grotesquely. They help the patient's skin grafts to heal flat and white. These are the braces and splints we make," he said, proudly demonstrating various shapes and sizes of splints that keep patients' arms and legs from twisting into deformed and useless shapes.

I watched him. I saw the pictures of his former patients on the wall. There were children who had been burned by abusive parents. There were deeply scarred victims of home explosions and automobile fires. There were adults caught in industrial accidents, burned as Ken Curtis had been burned. There was a wall of snapshots and with each picture a note of thanks. I didn't know that first week how often I would thank Bob Schneider for what he and his occupational therapists did for my son and the price they had to pay to do it.

"No! No! No!" David would scream when Bob came into his room. "You make me sick," he would sob as Bob approached his bed with the raw material to shape another brace, or with hands outstretched to manipulate and stretch David's arms and legs back into place.

Once I understood that the war between my son and his therapist was a just war, I gripped the chair and held back the heartbreak I felt every time David cried and struggled in pain. Many times I would have to leave the room in tears.

"No!" David cried again. "I won't do it. I won't do it. Mommy!" he screamed at me. "Mommy, he's hurting me."

Sometimes Bob simply worked in silence, saying nothing. Other times he coaxed and cajoled, pleaded and bribed. Other times he tried to explain gently and carefully why the process was necessary. Sometimes he just yelled back.

"Cut it out, Davie," he would say. "Knock it off!" Or, "Grow up! What do you think you are, a six-year-old? Act your age. You aren't two, you know."

Bob knew the treatments hurt but he refused to give in to David's loud complaints.

"Your son is going through hell," he told me once in the hall outside David's room. "He is experiencing pain more intense than most of us will ever know. But if we give in to that pain, we will destroy him."

One day Bob pointed out a young girl being wheeled into his occupational-therapy room. She was crippled and bent. Her neck strained downward. Her chin seemed to rest on her chest. Her arms were folded helplessly in her lap.

"See that?" he said in a pained whisper. "She was doing fine until they took her home. Now look at her."

"What happened?" I asked.

"Her parents gave in," he said. "They couldn't stand her cries of pain and discomfort. So they stopped the treatments and her body simply tucked in upon itself. Look at her. Now they want us to begin again. I hope it isn't too late," he added. "Too many times if you let it go even for a few days, the damage is irreversible."

Bob yelled at my son because he cared about his future. Day by day, he walked that long hallway to David's room, knowing the cries of anger and pain awaiting him there. Day by day, he was cheerful but persistent in manipulating my child's burned body back into life again. Day by day, he fit new splints and gently forced David's arms and legs, neck, and even his lips back into place.

Early in David's exercise program, Reggie Jackson stopped by again. He talked to David about his exercises. David had been protesting them loudly when Reggie walked into the room.

"I won't do the exercises," David said angrily, just as his famous friend walked into the room.

"What do you mean, David?" Reggie asked.

"I'm not doing those exercises anymore," David said, turning away from everyone in the room, even Reggie.

"Look at me, David," Reggie said. "Do you know how I got these muscles? Do you know how I got big and strong enough to hit those home runs and break those bats?"

Slowly, Davie rolled back to face the champion.

"I got them by exercise. My friends and I exercise every day. If we didn't, we would not make the team. If you want to be big and strong, you're going to have to do your exercises just like all the rest of us."

It was a lesson David remembered.

One afternoon, David was wheeled on a gurney from his room to Bob's therapy area in a refurbished wooden building in the rear of the UCI Medical Center.

"Hi, David," Bob said cheerily. "Ready to play a game?"

David hated Bob during those first few weeks of treatment. "You make me sick," he answered.

I knew Bob didn't like being hated any more than anyone else does, but he refused to be intimidated or scared off.

"Let's play catch," he said to David, picking up a large beach ball and preparing to throw it in David's direction.

David's fingers had been removed. His arms were in splints that left them about as mobile as two railroad semaphores. His arms swung back and forth in front of him like those of a cymbal player in a marching band.

"I can't catch it," David said. "Don't throw it."

Bob threw the ball and it bounced off David's chest. David got angry. "Don't throw it again!" my six-year-old son shouted at his therapist.

Bob threw it again. Again it bounced off David's body, this time almost knocking him to the floor.

David looked as if he was going to cry. Bob threw the ball again. This time, instead of trying to catch it, Davie used the stiff, braced arm to hit the beach ball hard.

The ball sailed through the air and hit Bob squarely on the head. He groaned and staggered about as though mortally wounded. David howled with laughter. Bob scrambled after the ball and threw it again. David hit the ball again, this time even harder.

"Just like Reggie," David muttered. "A home run."

"Just like Reggie," Bob replied.

Every day Bob, nurses Dee Fraser, Geri Chambers, and others would work on David's range-and-motion exercises.

"Okay, Davie, it's time for range and motion again," Dee would say, entering the room.

"No, Dee!" David cried. "Not today, please."

"What do you mean, not today?" she answered. "Range-and-motion exercises are every day."

David arched his back and groaned. "No, they aren't." He was tired. I could see he wanted to scream at her.

Dee sat down beside him. Gently she took one scarred and healing wrist in both her hands and bent it back as far as it would safely go.

"That's far enough," she said cheerily, watching David blink back the tears. "Let's count."

"One-two-three-four-five—" David started the countdown. Then he stopped. "Please, Dee, no more!" he cried.

"Count," she said firmly.

"Six-seven-eight-nine-ten!" he yelled at her.

Faithfully, nurses, therapists, and I worked David through his range-and-motion exercises. His body was always trying to contract. And we were always stretching those appendages back into place.

David still hadn't walked since the tragedy. His feet were still open. If he even tried to balance on them for a second it would cause him excruciating pain. He could only sit up on his gurney for several minutes, stretching that newly grafted back, before his eyes would fill with tears and he would beg to lie back down again.

The nurses had to ease and bribe and order David to exercise his body. They would help him sit up a little more each day. Five minutes became ten. Ten minutes became twenty. David would cry with pain and beg them to let him lie down again. He would shout angry words. He would threaten and he would pout. He would scream and cry and beg. Still they exercised him. One hour became two. Two hours became three. Little by little David was beginning to move again.

Finally, they had to get my son to walk. His feet had been totally burned. Even to stand on them was a nightmare.

"Time to walk, Davie," Dee Fraser said one day. "But first do you want to hear your tape?"

Davie liked the Rolling Stone tune "Start Me Up."

"Yes," David whispered, caught off guard. He loved for Dee to close the door and play his tapes so loud that the whole hospital staff would come running. He loved to see her dance about the room, teasing him, stretching him, getting him to sit up and move slowly with the rhythms.

"Let's dance," she said this time, lifting David off his bed and placing him gently on his feet for the first time.

"No!" David cried, fighting back the tears. His legs turned purple. He yelled with pain. But he stood there for several seconds, balancing on his own, blood rushing into his feet and legs. The music played. Doctors and nurses gathered just outside to watch as David took his first faltering step.

"Hurrah for you," Dee said, lifting him back to his bed. "You are a wonder."

"I hate you," David said. Then he threw his arms around her neck and began to cry tears of love and gratitude.

One lunchtime, Dee and David saw a maintenance man abandon his big chrome scrubber just outside David's room.

"I'll bet I can run that thing," Dee said.

"I'll bet you can't," David taunted back.

They both leaned out the door and looked up and down the hall until the corridor was empty. Then, quickly, Dee ran for the machine with David watching from his gurney in the doorway.

"How do you start it?" she whispered.

"Push something," he whispered back.

With a loud roar, the scrubber came to life. Dee somehow got it into drive and the next thing they knew, she was scurrying down the hospital hall behind a runaway machine.

"Stop it," David said, manipulating his gurney out into the hallway.

"I can't!" Dee shouted back. Somehow she managed to turn the fast-moving machine in Davie's direction. It was stuck in drive and aimed right at Davie's gurney.

"Look out!" she yelled, trying to keep her patient from being run over by the cleaning machine bigger than he and his gurney were together.

"Yow!" David yelled, as it hit the wall beside him and banged on down the hallway toward a crowd of doctors and nurses just turning the corner in their direction.

"Let's get out of here," David said, worriedly. "We're really in big trouble."

Back in the safety of David's room, Dee said, *"We're* not in trouble, Davie. *I'm* in trouble. You're not to blame," she said as the maintenance man ran up to turn off the cleaning machine. Almost without a pause, David said, "But the *fire* was my fault."

Dee caught her breath. "David, the fire wasn't your fault. You were the victim, not the bad guy."

"But I was there," he said sadly.

"You were asleep," she reminded him. "Only the guy who lights the fire is guilty of it."

For some strange reason, David had been struggling with guilt about the fire. Little by little we began to learn that just below the terrible burns were other scars, deeper hurts waiting to be healed.

Later, when another nurse accused them both of being in trouble for the runaway cleaning machine, David answered quickly, "Dee was

137

driving. I'm not guilty." Dee winked at Davie and whispered. "That's right."

As David's condition stabilized, the nurses used every trick they knew to help him become more active. Every little move he made hurt him terribly. His joints were stiff. His skin was tight. He didn't want to do anything but lie still. That was normal. Several times a week the nurses pushed him around the hospital grounds on his gurney. They made him go for rides when he wanted to stay safely and painlessly in his bed.

Dee Fraser and I were given the task of pushing David about the hospital grounds. Slowly David began to enjoy those times outside his room. He was discovering that his body was together again. He could move it. And though it gave him great pain, he was excited to realize that his body was beginning to function again.

The times outside the room brought another painful discovery to me. Everyplace we wheeled David, people stopped and stared. I tried to hide their surprised looks and stupid remarks from my son. "Look at that poor kid," one would say. "Oh, my gosh, look at that," another remarked. I felt angry and uncomfortable for my son. Dee told me to look straight ahead when they stared at him. "Pay no attention," she instructed me.

"Isn't it bad enough that David has to suffer the burns?" I answered. "Why should they make him suffer more?" David had been making such wonderful progress. I was afraid that people's responses would drive him back into his room and into a shell of embarrassment and anger. I wanted to protect him from every gawking stranger, from every crude and tasteless remark. There was no way. There never would be. The horror of that reality almost did me in. I wanted to yell at people when they passed: "Look him in the eye and smile as you would at any little child or turn your head and pretend you do not see, but don't just stare and mumble insults at him." "How could people be so thoughtless?" I asked Dee time and time again. "How could they stare at him? Don't they know that he can see their looks and hear their comments?"

"David's scars are their problem. They have to deal with it," she answered. "Our job is to get him out into the world again and not let anybody get in our way."

There were wild cats that lived around the fringes of the hospital. On one of their trips, Dee and David discovered the cats. David still had open areas where there had been no grafts or the grafts had not yet taken hold. These open areas were covered with Silvadene dressing and net bandages.

"Can we go see the cats today?" David begged Nurse Geri Chambers as they passed her in the hall.

"Okay, David, but don't touch them," she demanded, looking closely at Dee to be sure she understood. "And don't let the cats touch him, either," she added, noting Dee's innocent smile.

"Mommy," David said at I came up from the cafeteria, "come with us to see E.T." He had nicknamed the strangest looking cat "E.T." from the popular film of that title. Together, the three of us went looking for E.T. and his friends.

We found E.T. and David begged to hold him. Dee and I couldn't resist. We covered him all the way to his chin with a large hospital blanket and then we placed E.T. in David's lap.

Geri Chambers rounded the corner at full tilt.

"Get that cat off David!" she yelled.

Dee and I jumped up off the lawn. E.T. sprang into the bushes and David moaned. "She caught us," he said. "We're in trouble this time."

I knew it wasn't simply an act of disobedience on Dee's part. She had grown so close to David and she wanted so badly for him to use his body that she was willing to take these risks along the way. Just to see David stretch out his own arms was a thrill for both of us. To see him try to use his amputated fingers to touch that furry creature made us want to cheer.

Often David and Dee would draw pictures together. He would bend his grafted wrist around the oversized crayon. Dropping it over and over again, he would strain to draw a normal-sized body; then, suddenly, on those normal arms he would draw two giant hands. His fingers had been amputated at the top joint. The remaining stubs had grown together in a maze of scar tissue. Often he would lie on his bed holding up what was left of his hands to the light, staring at them in silence.

"When will my fingers grow back?" he asked Ken Curtis one painful day. Ken turned away. He couldn't speak.

"He will use those hands again," Bob Schneider promised us all. "Wait and see."

Day after day, Bob and his team of therapists worked David's wrists and hands. Day after day, David cried and wanted to end the torturous exercises. Bob persisted. David had no choice. Then one afternoon, Bob scattered M & M candies on a tray before his young patient.

"Eat them," he told David, and walked away.

"I can't, Bob," he whined. "Help me."

"Not this time, kid," Bob answered. "You do it."

David looked at those flat, circular candies on the metal tray. Then he began to stir them with his fist. Gradually he tipped one candy on its side and balanced it there. With one palm, he forced that single M & M onto the other hand. Slowly, carefully, he raised his palm into the air and tilted it just enough. The M & M fell into David's mouth. Bob yelled and grabbed David in his arms. David glowed with pride. This was no game that Bob was playing. This was hard work for both of them, but together they would win their battle. David would use his hands again.

One bright afternoon in May, for reasons still unknown, David asked Bob to help him make a present for me.

"What would you like to make your mom?" Bob asked. David didn't know.

"Just a present," he said. "A pretty present."

For a moment, Bob thought. Then he hurried away briefly and returned with string and beads. I had not arrived at the hospital yet and had no idea of the miracle that was about to take place.

"Here, David," Bob said, "let's string your mom a necklace."

Later, Bob told me how Davie looked at the string lying before him and at the colorful beads rolling about the tray.

"I can't do that, Bob," he answered. "Can I?"

"Yes, Davie, you can," Bob answered, kneeling down on the floor beside my son.

"Hand me the string, then," David said.

"Pick it up yourself," Bob answered.

"I can't," David fired back. "I can't pick up a string with no fingers. I can't make a necklace with no hands."

"Try, kid," urged the therapist.

Slowly, David began to fish around for the string. He became impatient and tried to quit. Bob stayed on his knees, encouraging him.

"Come on, you can do it," he said, over and over again.

"I can't!" David cried. "It's too hard."

"Try, Davie," Bob pleaded. And Davie tried. Bead after beautiful bead was strung on that long, hemp string. Some missed and went rolling across the floor. Once the whole string dropped and every hard-strung bead had to be strung again.

"I can't," David said again and again.

"You can," Bob answered each time, smiling.

When I arrived at the hospital that day, I found Davie and Bob in a rather coconspiratorial pose, grinning up at me from the floor of the therapy room.

"How goes it?" I asked innocently.

"Okay," David answered, his hand behind his back. Then he looked up at Bob as though waiting for a cue.

"Go on," Bob said, "show her."

"I have a present for you, Mommy," David said, grinning now and looking up at me. He had no ears, no hair, no eyebrows, and almost no nose. But his smile lit up the room for me. And when he held out his hand with that beautiful bead necklace hanging from it, I thought I would die from the pride I felt in my son that day.

"Oh, David, it is beautiful," I cried, tears streaming down my face.

"I made it, Mom," he said. "I made it all by myself."

I took him in my arms and tried to stop the tears. "Good boy, Davie," I said. "Good boy."

I looked down at the child in my arms and then across the room where Bob was waiting. I smiled at him. It wasn't enough. I still wonder if he knows how grateful I felt that day for what he, Dr. Achauer, the other doctors, nurses, and therapists had done—first, to save my son's life, and now, to give him hands again.

13

The first one hundred days of treatment had ended. David was well enough to be transferred to the Shriners Children's Hospital in Boston, just an hour by airplane from our home. The time had come to say good-bye to our new friends in Southern California. It wasn't easy.

"Ken's Lincoln is parked just outside the back entrance," Officer Branum advised us. "We'll hurry Davie down the rear elevator and try to get him past the crowd of reporters. Too much delay and that plane for Boston will leave without you."

"Oh, we're going to miss you all," I said to the nurses who had gathered to say good-bye. "I'm sorry I was such a witch," I apologized to one night nurse who had really felt my wrath.

The nurses laughed in chorus. For almost one hundred days I had cried, yelled, begged, questioned, demanded, and hounded each of them on David's behalf. And though, at the end, I saw the nurses as dear and committed friends, there were times along the way when we wondered if we would survive each other's strengths. After all the trouble I had made for them, I was really gratified to read what Sue Martinez, Davie's head nurse, said to a reporter from the *Los Angeles Times* after we had gone. "Marie was a big factor in her son's recovery," she told the reporter. "She's a tremendous woman with a lot of inner strength." Her words made me feel glad that I had fought to stay at Davie's side and grateful that those I fought had understood.

Davie's room was filled with lollipops and red and orange balloons that one nurse had brought to brighten up this sad farewell occasion. David wore a warm-up jacket another nurse had given him. Few words were spoken. In fact, Sue Martinez, who had done so much to set the pace for David's rehabilitation, refused to say good-bye. Instead, she said her regular "good morning" and hurried away on her busy rounds. Later I read in that same *Los Angeles Times* article that, speaking for the hospital staff, she had said, "It's going to be real lonely around here without David and Marie. It's going to take some getting used to, not having them here anymore."

Bob Schneider, David's wonderful occupational therapist, told the same reporter, "I thought about coming in this morning to say good-bye, but it would have been really hard. . . . We were special friends. At first we didn't think that he would live, but then we saw him overcome all these tremendous obstacles. We saw him make such remarkable gains and progress. We watched in awe as he got better and better. Now, having him go somewhere else is difficult."

Like Bob, many of our special friends on the staff of the UCI Medical Center and the Buena Park Police Department stayed away that morning so that they would not have to say good-bye. I scurried about the hospital on that last day fighting back the tears and asking myself over and over again why I was leaving this wonderful place to take Davie to the Children's Hospital in Boston for his next round of treatments.

The answer was simple. I was homesick. My fiancé was three thousand miles away. He had used up every bit of his vacation time to fly back and forth across the country to visit David and me. I called him almost every night from Ken and Judy's house and often, during those trying days, from the hospital for comfort and advice. I wanted to be nearer to him. And I wanted to get back to work again. The partners at my office and my boss, Mr. Scarin, had promised me a job upon my return from this nightmare vigil. My employer's insurance plan was paying hundreds of thousands of dollars for David's hospital bills. I needed and wanted to keep that job. My family and my handful of friends were in and around New York. Boston was so much closer to home.

"The press really wants to talk to you, Marie," Terry Branum said as Judy, Nurse Geri Chambers, and I wheeled David toward Ken's car.

"I'll talk to them," I answered. "Why not? They've really been wonderful to Davie and to me."

In a press conference two days before, I had tried to express my thanks to the media and to the Buena Park police, especially Officers Branum, Hafdahl, Skaugstad, Woofter, and Flanagan for their support. Terry presented me with a check for $102,000 collected from people around the nation who had read about Davie's tragedy. That money represented most of the fund that would be administered by the Buena Park Police Department on David's behalf. Ken and Judy Curtis and John sat on one side of me during the crowded press conference. Terry Branum sat on the other. Cameras and microphones, reporters' pens and pencils, recorded every word I said on this farewell to the wonderful people of Southern California.

"I want to thank God for my son's recovery," I told them. "And I want to thank all the people who have been praying for him during these last critical one hundred days." I looked at Ken and Judy Curtis sitting there, smiling at me. I remembered the long nights, the terror-ridden days, and their constant support.

"My faith has grown during this ordeal," I told the assembled reporters. "Without God I don't know how I would have gotten him through."

I didn't know what else to say. Reporters seem to have a tendency to think that thanking God for His help is just the expected thing to do. They don't seem to really believe you when you credit God or His people for getting you through a tragedy. But I said it anyway and hoped that someone understood how much I meant each word.

When they asked me about David's father, I answered, "David will have a love-hate feeling for a long time." Then I confessed my own mixed feelings about Charles. "I feel sorry for him. He still has to face what he's done for the rest of his life." When they asked about David's attitudes, the long-term effects of this, his father's crime on David, I replied, "David will never be the same. But he is a very courageous little boy. I think he will come through this."

For a moment, we stood near Ken's car talking one last time to the media before our flight to Boston. Several reporters would be accompanying us on the journey. The airport was an hour away. The scheduled American Airlines jet was due to depart in ninety minutes. We had to hurry.

I looked one last time at the UCI Medical Center, remembering when the police car rushed John and me from the airport to this same place to see my burned and bleeding son. Now we were returning to that airport on the first step of the journey home. Policemen who had guarded us stood on the fringes of the crowd. One told a reporter, "I feel so sad seeing David and Marie drive away. It's like seeing a good friend leave." I looked up to that third-floor Burn Center where Sue Martinez, her staff, and most of our hospital friends were already working with other burn victims and their families. "It's always difficult to say good-bye," Sue had said, "but this one was the hardest."

As we drove away, one reporter wrote that David looked like he was dressed for a Halloween party. He was wearing Reggie's baseball hat and was covered from head to foot with gauze. He wore a face mask with holes for his eyes and nose. David, trapped in that white, skintight wrapping, was hot and miserable and itching so badly he cried from the pain.

We were escorted quickly through the airport and on board the first-class section of a nonstop flight to Boston. David listened to the conversations between the pilots and the L.A. Airport control tower. He was propped up in a first-class aisle seat. When he wasn't itching, he was sleeping. He slept through breakfast, lunch, and the in-flight movie. It was David's first time out of a hospital for more than three months. He was still carrying a tenacious blood infection and ran a slight fever. Occasionally he awakened on the flight to sip a cold drink or ask us to scratch him more. Then he would fall asleep again. It was good he slept. He would need his strength for the wild, enthusiastic, almost runaway welcome we were to receive at Boston's Logan Airport.

Immediately upon landing, a Massachusetts State Trooper boarded the plane to warn us of the crowd of reporters, photographers, and television crews who had gathered to record our arrival. David wanted to be wheeled through the airport in a wheelchair. The police insisted he lie flat on a gurney on his way to the waiting ambulance. David cried. The police persisted. I was beginning to fear this entire Boston adventure. My fears were justified.

The police helped our nurse, Geri Chambers, strap David onto the gurney. Then we turned to face the crowd. It was unbelievable. Reporters pressed in on us in such a rush that I was separated from David by the mob and locked out of his ambulance.

"I'm his mother!" I yelled above the noise of the jostling reporters and the applauding public. "Let me through!"

If David hadn't been strapped to the gurney, he might have been trampled in the crowd. I was afraid we both would die under their stampeding feet. Even in my panic, I was appreciating the crowd-control abilities of the Buena Park police and of Officer Terry Branum's

145

professional handling of the press. In Boston, we faced them alone. Through no fault or decision of ours, David had become a celebrity. The story of a boy almost burned to death by his father was still making headlines around the world. David had become a symbol of all the innocent, suffering children who had been abused. In fact, child abuse had become the number-one American family nightmare and David was unofficially its cover story.

Shriners Children's Hospital in Boston was an oasis for David and me after that mob welcome to Boston. The first and second floors of the three-story red brick building are the Shriners Burns Institute's offices and research labs. The third floor houses the patient facility. There are only eighteen beds, but the Institute is reputed to be one of the finest burn-treatment centers in the world. David was sponsored by generous Shriners. His treatment at their Institute did not cost us a penny. The Burns Institute is not really a hospital but a special center for burn treatment connected by a long underground tunnel to the huge Massachusetts General Hospital nearby.

Maureen Byrne, believe it or not the real name of the Institute's head nurse, welcomed us.

"You are going to like it here, David," she said. And the bouquet of balloons drifting by overhead with WELCOME, DAVIE banners supported her promise. The ward is bright with color. Sunlight streams in the windows. Cartoon characters dance around the walls. Winnie-the-Pooh stands looking down on the children, his honey jar in hand. Snow White and the seven dwarfs march by with Mickey and Minnie Mouse in tow. In the middle of the large room is a nursing station and eighteen beds fanning out around it. Each bed has a television set and a cartoon character nearby. Windows bring in the light and let the children look out at the world they soon must enter. There is a beautiful therapy room nearby with building blocks, stuffed toys, art easels, and video games where therapists reinvigorate joints and stretch muscles of the newly grafted children.

Geri helped David settle into his new hospital home. She took off his mask. His face was red and wrinkled. His lips were swollen. He was sweaty and miserable from the five-hour journey. The evening nursing supervisor, Jane Bell, told us that doctors would take twenty-four hours to examine David and evaluate his medical needs before commenting on his condition or scheduling the reconstructive surgeries he would receive there.

Late that night I still hadn't talked to a doctor at the Burns Institute.

A social worker suggested that I leave David behind and return to New York within the week.

"Get on with your life," she told me. "Go to New York. Start back to work. Treat David as if he isn't different from any other child."

I paced my Boston boarding-house room, her words cluttering up my resolve to stay with David through this whole long process of healing. Again I had to make a difficult decision. Were these hospital personnel just trying to get rid of me as the UCI personnel had tried at first? Would David feel abandoned and alone? Would my presence guarantee the kind of attention I thought he needed and deserved? Or would this temporary move away from my son be necessary to help him become more independent? Would the risk of leaving him now be doing him a favor in the long haul?

I battled the questions back and forth. Although David still couldn't walk, I thought the danger to his life had ended. The bulk of his treatment would involve reconstructive and rehabilitative therapy. I thought they would just spend the time stretching his joints and applying pressure to his scars through the newly fitted Jobst suit. I knew they would continue splinting him. They would fight the ongoing infections, but the infections seemed tame now by comparison to the UCI infections we had battled. My son was almost totally grafted. Unfortunately, David's neck had pulled downward. His head rested on his chest. He had to lean backward to look up at the balloons above his bed. Dr. Achauer had told me that the first surgery would be to release his neck. It would be a critical operation, but he assured me that the surgeons in Boston could handle it. Besides, they promised that there was one nurse on duty in the institute for every young patient, twenty-four hours a day. And if the social worker was right, perhaps it was time for me to begin my life again and leave David on his own for a while. She was wrong.

On the day before his seventh birthday, doctors in Boston wheeled my son into the operation theater for a three-hour surgery on his neck. They successfully released his neck from the tuck-down position with a new skin graft. He didn't look old and bent anymore. His bottom teeth and gums no longer protruded from his lower lip. In fact, his lips began to look quite normal again. The hospital's director of Social Services announced to the press that David had "sailed through his last major surgery." I was relieved and grateful.

During those first few weeks at Shriners, I saw David take his first painful steps alone. He shuffled about his tiny room, rocking back and forth as he moved those tight, scar-covered legs on his own. A therapist attached a special metal device to David's arm so that he could feed himself. Everyone, including myself, was very encouraged by David's progress.

Because of David's blood infection, he had been kept in isolation from his future playmates in the Burns Institute. The day before his successful neck surgery, the nurses threw an outdoor surprise birthday party for my son. Outside, in the fenced playground area on the hospital grounds in downtown Boston, there was no need to isolate David. He was wheeled onto the playground surrounded by cheering children. He was still wrapped in gauze and wearing his protective mask. Most of the other children had suffered burns on 10 to 20 percent of their bodies. One little girl wore a face mask like Davie, but most of the children were far less seriously burned than he was.

Performing clowns joined the group and entertained as David and his new friends ate ice cream and cake, baked by nurses for the occasion. David laughed a lot that day. His brown eyes sparkled through the tiny holes in his mask. He opened a pile of presents. He especially liked a robot toy and Simon, a musical computer game.

David received hundreds of letters from well-wishers across the country. The people of Massachusetts who had read about his arrival in Boston sent hundreds and hundreds of birthday cards. One letter was especially exciting for David. The stationery had "The White House" imprinted in blue letters. Apparently even the president and his wife had seen David on television during our flight from California. The president wrote, "I think your California Angels' cap suits you fine." Later, in the long and thoughtful letter, the president said, "We will pray for you and hope that every day you'll feel better. Hang in there, David!" Enclosed were beautiful pictures of the White House and Air Force One and a book describing the White House.

Unfortunately, in spite of the first successful surgery and the excitement of arriving in Boston as celebrities, we missed our friends from Southern California. David cried himself to sleep several nights missing special people from UCI like Dee or Geri, Bob or Sue. I thought often of our friends and how much they had done for both of us. I thought that in Boston we would be closer to our old friends and family. In fact, I thought that by moving east my problems would end. I wanted to be nearer to John, but I saw him less. My family was only two hundred miles away now but I saw them less and less. Although we were closer by thousands of miles, the distance between us seemed longer and more difficult to cross.

Suddenly, from that warm, loving environment I had discovered in Buena Park, I was back in the big city where nobody knew me. My son was in a hospital where, in spite of my protests, they would only allow me to stay a few hours a day. At night I had to go back to a lonely boarding house. I was petrified by the strange city and the dark and lonely streets. I hated eating in restaurants by myself.

In California I had the UCI staff, the Buena Park police, and members of the Eastside Christian Church. I especially had Ken and Judy. I always had the Curtis family when I returned from the hospital at night. I always had someone to talk to about my day and how it went. When David was in trouble, they would speed to the hospital to pray with me. When I was screaming at hospital or police personnel, they would know how to calm me down and get communications going again. But in Boston, I was alone.

At UCI, when I did shout at doctors or nurses, they seemed to understand my stress. They worked to hear me. They tried to be reasonable about my questions and complaints. They tried to meet my requests and to help me understand when I was confused or ignorant. It was not true in Boston. I was grateful for the Shriners' generosity, but I seldom saw the doctors in that place. They hardly spoke to me. The surgeons were like aliens living somewhere on a distant planet. Now and then my son would be beamed up to that planet without warning or explanation. Often I didn't know when or why he was being treated. My anxiety was growing more intense each day.

Worse, my faith was still in its infancy. It wasn't natural yet for me to grab hands with strangers and pray. I wasn't good at finding what I needed or wanted to read in the Scriptures. Judy had given me a beautiful Bible (and David had been sent dozens of them by well-wishers across the country), but I stopped regular study of the Word when Ken and Judy weren't waiting for me at home or Judy's Bible-study group wasn't there to encourage and instruct me. I even quit going to church on Sunday. It happened before I noticed. I didn't know anyone in Boston to ask about churches. I looked through the Yellow Pages and on an announcement board near my boarding house, but I couldn't decide among all the denominational choices and I still wasn't in the mood for high church liturgy. I missed my Eastside Christian friends. I missed their hugs, their prayers, their words of encouragement.

And though I missed them, I didn't try to find another group of Christians to join in worship while we stayed in Boston. It was a serious mistake.

Ken and Judy encouraged me to find a church to attend in Boston. They even recommended specific churches to consider when David and I returned to New York. What they knew and I didn't know was that my spirit would begin to tuck down into its fetal position without spiritual exercise, just as David's body wanted to turn in on itself when he wasn't working to prevent it.

David seemed to be making wonderful progress, but I had a growing and ominous sense that something was about to go wrong and that I was not equipped to handle the new crisis, whatever it might be.

At the same time, I came down with a severe case of bronchitis. I suppose my exhaustion and loneliness made me vulnerable to the virus. Hospital personnel advised me to quarantine myself from David, to go back home to Brooklyn, and to get some rest and recuperation time for myself. It was the first time since his tragedy that I had left my son. I ignored my own intuition and went to Brooklyn. I returned within the week no longer contagious and somewhat rested. As I sat with his therapist by David's bed, a new doctor approached.

"Hi," he said cheerily, introducing himself as David's anesthesiologist and sitting down beside us.

"What are you doing here?" I asked, knowing that an anesthesiologist would not just drop by for a visit.

"I've come to talk about Davie's surgery tomorrow," he said.

"What surgery tomorrow?" I asked, coming straight up off the bed. I turned to the therapist, who had been working on David's hands. "What are they going to do to him?" I asked.

"First time I've heard," he answered. "David's hands were supposed to be next."

"We're operating on his head," the doctor answered.

"His head?" I said. "What are you going to do to his head?"

David began to whine. I knew I should never have these clinical discussions with him present. But sometimes I just blundered in anyway.

"I want hair," he whimpered. "Don't let them graft my head."

Somehow David had heard that once the open spots on the skull were grafted, hair would not grow. David hated being bald when all the other children had hair. He began to cry loudly, "I want hair! Don't let them graft me."

"Davie, honey," I said, trying to undo what I had already done, "you have to think about getting well.' We'll get you hair. Don't worry."

The anesthesiologist tried to explain that David's head was still an open area. He still had a pesky staph infection. They were afraid it would grow worse. He was already running a temperature and they didn't want to take the risk of even more infections in his blood.

"It's a very minor surgery," the anesthesiologist promised. "It will be over in no time and," he said to David, "I will guarantee that you will not feel a thing."

The next morning David was scheduled for surgery at 8:00 A.M. I waited with him until 10:00 A.M. He grew more and more worried. I grew more and more tense. Finally, they took him to the preoperating area and tried to put him to sleep. Nothing worked. David was crying. I patted him gently and promised that I would stay beside him until he went to sleep. I even carried him to the operating table and placed him on it. I hugged him and tried to relax him. Finally, he slept. As I walked away from my tiny son, I began to sob.

"Don't worry, Mrs. Rothenberg," they said to me, "this is an easy surgery. We'll take good care of him. Don't cry."

I cried anyway. Every time I left David in the operating room, I was a basket case. My sister Clarissa came to be with me that day. She went to get us coffee while I waited. The surgery was scheduled for thirty minutes. Sixty minutes passed. Still there was no word. David had been in surgery ninety minutes when I walked upstairs and saw his bed still empty in the hallway.

"Is Davie out?" I asked a nurse.

"No," she answered, "but you had better go downstairs and wait. We don't allow the parents up here during surgery."

I angrily obeyed. I stalked to a telephone. I called my sister Sandra just to share my anger and my growing fear.

"Mrs. Rothenberg?" A resident appeared behind me. I hung up the phone and turned to face him.

"What's wrong?" I asked. "What's wrong with Davie?"

"We had to stop the surgery," he explained matter-of-factly.

"What do you mean, you had to stop the surgery?" I shouted at him.

Startled by my outburst, he laughed and tried to shrug away the seriousness of the surgical abort.

"What's wrong with Davie?" I asked.

"We just had to stop," he said glibly. "He's in his room."

"I want to see him," I demanded. "Now!"

"Well," he hesitated, "they're getting him settled and as soon as he's settled, we'll bring you up."

For what seemed like endless hours I waited for them "to settle" my son. I knew something serious had gone wrong. The doctor patronized me. He had spoken to me as though I were a child. I had spent the last months by Davie's side, struggling to see him through every treatment, major or minor. At UCI, I had demanded and received honest answers. I refused to quietly accept anybody's glib explanation when it came to the well-being of my son.

Finally, the doctor entered the waiting room accompanied by the head nurse and two social workers. They asked me to follow them to the family room. My heart was pounding. I expected the worst.

"Mrs. Rothenberg," the doctor began, "we've had some problems."

"What kind of problems?" I asked, barely holding back my rage.

"Shortly after your son was anesthetized, his blood pressure dropped precariously. His heart stopped beating and he stopped breathing entirely."

"Is David dead?" I asked, gripping my sister's hand.

"No," the doctor answered, "we revived him quickly, but we don't know yet what or how permanent the damage will be."

"What did you do to my baby?" I cried. "You've ruined my baby." I flew into a rage. I don't remember all I said or threatened that day but it was considerable, I am sure. I couldn't believe we had come through the last one hundred days just to lose David because of minor surgery. Dr. Achauer had assured me David was in excellent condition. These doctors had promised that the surgery would be minor, "thirty minutes at most." Now this!

"What happened?" I finally stammered.

"We don't know," they replied.

"You don't know?" I yelled. "You don't know?"

Again I began to scream. I was shaking. I was about to throw up. My sister was crying. The social workers kept asking me if they should phone John.

"I want to see my baby!" I yelled at them over and over again. "I want to see my baby."

Finally, they relented and took me to him. After the moment I first saw Davie in the Burn Center in California, this moment was the worst moment of my life. Davie was lying on his bed. His eyes stared straight ahead without seeing. His body twitched occasionally. There was no other movement. He looked dead to me. He was only semiconscious. I stared at my son.

"Oh, Davie, Davie," I cried, "what have they done to you?"

I ran from the room. The moment the door closed behind me, I began to scream. The resident's first warning had been glib and sarcastic. The doctor's explanation had been short and without compassion. The shock was terrible. Seeing him lying there after all we had been through almost unnerved me permanently. The social worker thought I was having a nervous breakdown. The doctors tried to explain. The minute Davie quit breathing, they had administered CPR (cardiopulmonary resuscitation) to his chest. He had been revived, they said, almost immediately. There should not be these first awful signs of permanent, long-range damage. But there were.

I ran to the phone and called John. Then I immediately dialed Ken and Judy in California.

"You have to pray," I shouted across the distance. "Davie is dying." They said they would come immediately. I told them to wait until we knew more. Then I took up vigil again beside David's bed. I felt guilty for letting this hospital staff chase me away for whatever reason. I felt as though I had failed my son. I had let the strangeness of this new situation intimidate me. Maybe there was nothing I could have done, but I felt terrible as I sat there watching him.

Apparently, his brain had swollen under the anesthesia. It remained enlarged. Even as he slowly regained consciousness, his eyes were dilated. He looked as though he could see images, shadows, but nothing more. He didn't see or recognize people. He couldn't speak. He drooled and wet his bed. Suddenly he began to shake. I screamed for the nurse. David had his first postoperative seizure. They called it "common" after such a brain trauma. More seizures followed. I watched and waited and prayed desperate prayers.

What happened to Davie in that operating room was worse than his burn, for my burned child with his beautiful brain could survive; but when his brain was threatened, when he reverted to infancy, I felt more fear for his future than I ever had before. His mind had been damaged. No one could say yet how severely. His personality was gone. The doctors dropped by with more and more complex theories to explain what had happened. My sister and I could not understand a word of it.

One afternoon, Sandra and I were walking through the streets of Boston. I saw the beautiful old brick buildings through a haze of tears.

We entered a bookstore. I found a heavy, five-inch-wide medical book called *The Textbook of Medicine* by Benson and McDermitt. I bought it and began to search for definitions. We read about the brain, about edema, about various anesthesias and their potential negative effects. I had to know what the doctors were talking about. We sat in a restaurant and flipped pages, desperately trying to find some clues to David's condition and what could be done about it. The hospital had refused to talk to the press. They were happy to have the media around when all was going well for my son. But when something went wrong, immediately they hid behind a "no comment."

I found a lot of information that day. I wrote notes and began to press the doctors for more information. David was my son. I had to know. I had to have some answers. Then I made an appointment with David's surgeon. I asked him endless questions. "What state was David in when I first saw him? What would you call it? Was he in a coma? What is edema on the brain and how was it caused? Is the brain still swollen? Why are you taking him off the medicine that treats the swelling? What will happen when he doesn't have it? What caused the seizures? How long will they last? If the swelling is gone, why can't he speak again? Why can he recognize people and objects some days and not recognize them other days? Should he be moved from the Institute to the neurological ward at Massachusetts General Hospital? Why can't you x-ray the brain to see what the damages are? How long must we wait?"

The doctor answered every question as best he could. They were in a terrible bind. They didn't know what had happened to Davie or why. They couldn't scan his brain because it was still open and needed grafting. That would risk further damage. All we could do was wait. They didn't know how long.

"What time limit are you setting?" I asked him. "I have to know."

"It could be weeks," he answered. "It could be months."

"I have to go to California for my ex-husband's sentencing," I said. "Will Davie be all right while I am gone?"

"We think so," he said. "We just have to wait and be patient."

This time, apparently, there was really nothing I could do to speed David's recovery. The nurses were working with him around the clock. The doctors had become very solicitous and were constantly conferring on David's case. And I felt determined to speak to the judge before my ex-husband received his sentence. There were rumors that because David hadn't died, Charles would be given a short sentence or a long parole. I had to speak a word on my son's behalf. John and I prepared for that awful return trip to California to appear before the court. On the day of our departure, I tried to say good-bye to my son.

"Davie," I said, looking down at my son, "Mommy's going to California." He was sitting in a wooden cart outside on the hospital grounds. His right arm twitched occasionally. There was no glimmer of recognition. He didn't look at me. He didn't even know I was speaking.

"Davie," I said loudly, "I'm going to see your daddy." Still David didn't move. There was no response.

"Good-bye, Davie," I cried. "Give Mommy a kiss, please, David."

He didn't move. There was no life in his eyes. Nothing.

My son was gone. First his body had been burned away. Now his brain seemed damaged beyond repair. I could not stop the tears.

"Good-bye, Davie," I sobbed. "Mommy will be back in just a few days. And remember that I love you."

14

Eleven days after his arrest in San Francisco, Charles was charged with attempted murder, arson, inflicting great bodily injury, and the use of a deadly weapon. He pleaded not guilty. His public defender, Ramon Ortiz, considered using "insanity" as Charles' defense but my ex-husband refused psychiatric testing. A preliminary hearing was scheduled in the Orange County Municipal Court. Deputy District Attorney Tom Avdeef had carefully prepared his case against Charles. Witnesses had been found and asked to appear. Appropriate evidence had been assembled. During the preliminary hearing, Charles could have had opportunity to examine the evidence against him, but he decided to forego that hearing altogether. He had already confessed to the police and reporters from the *Los Angeles Times* that he had attempted to kill David. He claimed that he had been despondent over the possibility that he might lose visitation rights with our son and that he was considering murder/suicide. In foregoing the preliminary hearing, Charles claimed he wanted to protect me from the trauma of testifying and to keep me from having to leave David's bedside in the UCI intensive-care unit. In another courtroom, he won the right to donate blood to David. I told reporters he could donate blood if he wanted but he's a positive blood type and David is negative. The blood wouldn't come directly to our son anyway.

April 27, seven weeks after Charles' arrest, I read headlines claiming that another Superior Court judge had granted Charles the right to visit David in the hospital on the condition that Dr. Achauer and I would approve the visit. The very idea terrified and distressed me.

April 28, twenty-four hours later, the same judge called a press conference to deny that he would allow Charles to visit David. "Under no circumstances," said the judge, "would I let someone visit, in a hospital, a victim he is accused of trying to kill."

May 6, before Superior Court Judge Donald McCartin, Charles again made his not-guilty plea. His defense attorney told reporters, "I think it's clear . . . that he has committed some crime. The question is what crime was it?" He added, "I do not think malice can be established in Mr. Rothenberg's mind at the time." He told reporters he was hoping to have the charges reduced to attempted manslaughter. That charge could reduce Charles' sentence for his crime against David by five years.

May 28, before Superior Court Judge James R. Franks, II, Charles tried to change his plea to guilty but only if he could withdraw the plea if David died and murder charges were filed. He said he would take any sentence the judge handed down, but Judge Franks refused to accept his guilty plea on those grounds.

June 25, Charles' guilty plea was accepted in the Orange County Superior Court by Judge Franks. In his change of plea, Charles read from a three-page letter he had written:

I know I have done a terrible thing. I can only hope and pray that David will someday forgive me. . . . What happened the night of March 2 will torture me for as long as I live. How I came to the point where I tried to take my son's life is unexplainable. I just snapped and did not realize what I had done until it was too late. I know it is hard for you to understand why and how a father who loves you so very much could do what I did. But I pray, as time goes by, through the grace of God, you will understand that I love you so much and I did not want to lose you. I know now that I was wrong. Please forgive me.

July 30, in the Orange County Superior Court, Judge Franks would sentence Charles for his crime. I had already written a four-page letter to the courts requesting that Charles be given the maximum sentence without parole for his crime. I requested that the judge and Charles be shown photographs of David taken after the fire. Now, I felt I had to appear at the sentencing for several significant reasons.

First, I had followed each stage of Charles' strange defense with growing fear. He had always been a clever con man. He knew how to protect himself with an elaborate and carefully acted series of lies, subtle innuendos, and symbolic "noble acts." He had stuck by his lie that he was afraid of losing visitation rights with David, even though there was not one shred of evidence to support that I had ever kept him from our son. He implied that my fiancé, John, and I were torturing him with our "exclusive" rights to David, when in fact, out of pity for Charles, we had consistently included Charles as a fourth member of our "family" when he was released from prison. Charles even waited to confess his crime until David had been taken off the critical list. He did not want to risk a confession if it would lead to a murder charge. In courtroom appearances, when the press was present, Charles looked humble and contrite. I did not trust our legal system to understand how cunning and dangerous my ex-husband could be. I was afraid that he would lie himself into a light sentence, lie himself into an early parole, and try to lie his way back into our lives again. It was a terrifying prospect. I wanted to be there at the sentencing to do my part to keep those fears from coming true.

There was a second reason that John and I risked leaving David semiconscious in the Burns Institute to fly across the country to be at Charles' sentencing. After his crime, Charles had it easy. Because he had been isolated in prison and the courts, he had not seen with his own eyes what his fire had done to our son. I was afraid the courts would not show him the pictures of David after he had been burned. I knew he would not see David lying semiconscious in the Children's Hospital with possible permanent damage to his brain. I was the only one who really knew the changes Charles' crime had made in our six-year-old boy. The district attorney told me that Charles often asked fearfully, "Is Marie going to be in the courtroom today?" He was afraid to look me in the eye. Because he didn't have to face David or me, he didn't have to face what he had done. I wanted him to face it. I wanted him to look me in the eye. I wanted him to realize in that look what he had done to both of us. Then, maybe, he could feel authentic grief for his terrible crime. Then, perhaps, David and I would be safe from further terror.

I had been a good and faithful wife to Charles. In return, he had broken every promise and commitment he had made to me. He had lied over and over again. He used me and my credit rating to steal from others. He had even stolen from me. From the beginning, he manipulated me with smooth words, innocent looks, heartfelt promises, and tearful confessions. Then, when I gave him another chance, he would lie and steal and cheat again.

I was not without fault. My personality can be abrasive. I am outspoken. I don't lie. I don't hide my feelings. That's the way I am. But Charles never had reason to hate me or to hate his son or even to hate John. Charles was a liar. And as I watched him bargain with judges and attorneys and manipulate the press, I could not sit silently by. I had taken all the subtle and violent abuse from this man that I would take. I refused to let him con the courts as he conned everybody else. I could not let them put him back on the streets again. I would not live with fear for myself and for David for the rest of our lives. Charles was an attempted murderer with a long record of crime and arrests and prison terms. My concerns were practical. I wanted to protect David and myself from further terror. I wanted a dangerous and cunning man put away. I did not seek revenge. I did not dwell on hatred. I just wanted justice done, and a life sentence without parole for the attempted murder of his son seemed just to me.

My knees were trembling as John and I entered Judge Franks' courtroom in Santa Ana, California. The room was crowded with spectators and the press. Dazed and trembling, I sat down on a crowded bench. John stood slightly behind me, his left hand resting on my shoulder.

Suddenly, a policeman led Charles into the courtroom. It was the first time I had seen him since he came to my apartment to take away our son. The entire room grew silent when Charles appeared. He was wearing prison overalls and a jail number. A rush of fear and anger almost overwhelmed me. I turned pale and began to shake. I gripped John's hand desperately. I grew dizzy. My eyes wouldn't focus. I was afraid I might faint.

When I saw Charles, my system reacted more intensely than when I saw David those first terrible times in the hospital. I had been strong then, strong enough to comfort and reassure my son. I was not strong in the courtroom.

I struggled to stop shaking. I swallowed hard. I tried to slow my panicked breathing and control my urge to faint. I stared at Charles. Sitting behind his attorney, my ex-husband stared down at the floor. The courtroom filled with words.

Charles' defense attorney was speaking. He asked the judge to consider "the nature of the man" before imposing a maximum sentence.

"This is a man raised in an orphanage without love and security," Charles' attorney told the court. "His son's birth was the most joyful event in his whole life."

My stomach knotted as I listened.

"How did this happen?" Charles' attorney asked rhetorically. "You have an emotion-packed situation created by a divorce-and-custody situation," he answered himself. "Both parties created the situation . . . both parties are victims."

I fought back my rage. Charles' attorney was searching for reasons to explain what could not be explained. He wanted Charles to receive a light sentence. Charles sat across the courtroom looking remorseful. How often I had seen that look.

"Charles Rothenberg," the attorney continued, "is a man with love for his child and also with the frailties and weaknesses of a human being."

Even as I stared with anger at my ex-husband, I knew I pitied him. He was a victim of his past. We are all victims of our past. But there is no one, not even Charles, who could blame his past suffering for the present suffering he had caused our son. Charles and I were both abused as children, but that gave us no right to abuse our children. There was no way for anyone to justify that awful crime against an innocent child, and I prayed that the court would not be tricked into excusing Charles as I had excused him so many times before. District Attorney Avdeef responded angrily to Charles' attorney's plea for leniency.

"The man had the intent to murder his child," District Attorney Avdeef said. "All the rest of this is baloney."

When Charles spoke, the courtroom was hushed.

"I'd like to now ask your forgiveness, Marie and John," he said, "as I now forgive you both. . . ."

I looked around the court, hoping people could see through that kind of confession. It was almost comical. There was no reason for him to forgive me or John. We had done nothing to offend or hurt him. He was not capable of real sorrow or real remorse. In his supposed act of forgiveness, he was subtly indicting us both as coconspirators to his crime.

Charles continued speaking to John and me. "I'd like you to take care of my beloved son, David," he said, dramatically.

He made it sound as though he were giving David to us as an act of sacrifice on his part. And though we had every reason to believe that David was much beloved by Charles, that same man had tried to murder our son and in his failure had left David permanently and tragically damaged.

The courtroom was silent as Judge Franks invited me to speak. The district attorney had asked me to tell the court exactly what Charles did to David and what the results in his young life would be. Cameras, reporters, spectators turned in my direction. At first, Charles looked away. Slowly, fearfully, he glanced over his right shoulder in my direction. His lips were tight, his eyes wide open and unblinking. He sat slightly hunched over in his chair.

I suppose he thought that I would say, "I forgive you." I had said it often enough in the past. I had been loyal to Charles. I stood by his side when he should have been abandoned. I accepted his abuse without deserving it. I had trusted him with my life and with the life of our son. Even after our divorce, I had tried to build a normal relationship among the three of us. I wanted David to feel good about his father. I wanted them to be close. But everything I had given him had been betrayed in this crime against our son. I could not forgive him. I would not forgive him until I felt his confession and his grief were real.

I told the court of the seriousness of David's burns. His face and most of his body had been burned away. Most of his fingers and his toes had been amputated. I told them how many times David had come close to death and that even while I spoke, he was lying in the Children's Hospital in Boston suffering brain damage from a recent grafting surgery mishap. I told them that David was only semiconscious, that he couldn't see or speak and that the doctors couldn't tell me if he would ever return to normal again. They didn't know how badly or permanently damaged his brain might be. I then looked Charles directly in the eyes. "David is afraid of him for this," I said clearly. "Every night before he goes to bed he fears that his father will come to kill him. David will never be a normal child again," I continued. "He will have scars, both physical and mental, for the rest of his life." Then, to the judge, I pleaded, "David needs peace in his life. He needs to be away from his father forever."

When I had concluded, Charles' defense attorney asked one last time for leniency. Then Judge Franks leaned forward at the bench and addressed the packed courtroom.

"Regarding Charles' story that he had planned to take his own life on the night he tried to murder David," the judge intoned, "a review of the facts would indicate that at no time did you ever intend to harm yourself at all. . . . You specifically intended to kill David."

That clear, Judge Franks pronounced the sentence.

"Charles Rothenberg, I sentence you to nine years for attempted murder, three years for willful intent to do great bodily injury, and a year for committing a felony within five years of a prior felony count." He paused and looked directly at my ex-husband.

"That sentence is not enough time for what you did," he said. "Because of a quirk in the law, thirteen years is the maximum I can give you. But that is far too low in my opinion for your crime." During the sentencing, Judge Franks was formal and correct. After the trial, the press reported that in the privacy of his chambers, he looked at Davie's burn pictures and "wept hard."

I had begged the court to give Charles a life sentence without chance of parole. In fact, Charles would be eligible for parole in only seven and one-half years (February 1990).

Then Charles was taken away and I stood to face the crowd of reporters waiting to question me. Once again I told them how Charles had turned the whole story around in jailhouse interviews with the press while I had been forced to keep silent because of the pending criminal case in the courts. Once again I told them it wasn't a custody battle, that Charles had equal access to David before the kidnapping and attempted murder. Once agan I explained why Charles should have been given a life sentence and that the sentence he had received was much too light for the crime he had committed and for the ongoing threat he posed for David and for me.

Even as I spoke, Charles was being driven back to prison. I don't know what was going through his mind. My anger and fear gave way to waves of grief. I felt sorry for everybody, for David, for myself, and even for Charles.

And I felt some peace again. For a moment, at least, we were free from the threat of further violence and we could get back to saving David's life and providing him with some kind of future. But always in the back of my mind would be the fear that when Charles was released from prison, what then? Would he call us on the telephone? Would he climb those stairs and knock on our door? Would he try to frighten or hurt us again? The courts are helpless. The police can do no more. We simply have to wait and wonder.

We returned to Boston. David was a patient in the Shriners Hospital there for more than one hundred days. Dr. Achauer had assured me that the institute is one of the finest burn-treatment centers in the world. Other authorities agreed. We met many wonderful, able, and loving professionals while we were there and we are grateful for all the good they did for David. But through one unexplicable mishap in that place, David suffered terrible loss.

After the disastrous anesthesia and aborted surgery, David couldn't see for more than a week. He couldn't speak for three weeks. And when he finally began to speak again, he couldn't remember even the simplest words. He slurred the words he did remember, and his motor skills were minimal at best.

"What do you want, Davie?" I said, feeling impatient and frustrated and angry that my son had been reduced to an infant once again. "Let Mommy help you."

"I want . . ." David stopped and looked around the room trying to remember the forgotten word.

"What?" I said again. "What do you want?"

"Mack," he stuttered. "Moke," he tried again.

"Milk, Davie?" I tried to help him. "Do you want milk?"

"Yes, moke," he said, unable to pronounce even so familiar a word.

"I'll get some," I said, rushing to get a pint of milk and a straw for my frustrated and thirsty child. When I returned, I put the straw up to Davie's lips. How many thousands of times he had drunk milk or cola or juice from a straw; this time he couldn't do it.

"Here, blow," I said, blowing air through my lips to demonstrate.

"Whwww . . ." David copied my blowing motion.

"Now, suck like this," I said, sucking in my cheeks and making a loud smacking noise with the straw.

Finally, David got the hang of it. His physiotherapist and I had to retrain him to use things so simple as a spoon or crayon. His speech therapist worked with him every day to help him regain his most basic childhood vocabulary. The psychologist tested David's age-level learning skills. His first tests showed him performing at the level of a small child. And David had always been above his grade level before the accident in Boston. But the therapists, the psychologist, and the nurses worked day and night to stimulate and retrain his brain. Little by little, David began to show signs of improvement.

Just before David's abortive surgery, Reggie Jackson made another surprise visit. He had seen David frequently in California, but since

David's transfer to the east coast, Reggie had not dropped by. Then, suddenly, he appeared at the Children's Hospital. Immediately, David's spirits soared. The champion sat on David's bed. They played Simon and talked batting averages and league wins and World Series prospects.

Finally, when Reggie moved away to visit other patients, David fell back on his bed, smiling broadly. "He came to see me again," he said, to the nurses, blinking back tears. "Reggie came, didn't he?"

"Yes," they said, "he came to see you again." And what a difference it made. Apparently it made a difference to Reggie, too. He told a single reporter who discovered him there that "looking at those kids and all they suffer makes even my .214 batting average look great.

"Visiting those kids," he said, shaking his head and wiping way the tears in his eyes, "makes you grateful that you can just go out and swing the bat at all."

Soon David was rapidly regaining lost skills. His memory improved markedly. He even began to practice the "burn ward shuffle," dragging his stiff, scarred legs off the bed and onto the floor for a few faltering steps about the room. Therapists created new splints to stretch and strengthen his limbs. He was measured and fitted for a skintight Jobst suit and face mask. He would have to wear this outfit, much like a surfer's wet suit, for at least a year. The Jobst suit, named after its inventor, put constant pressure on David's skin. The pressure helped keep gruesome and discolored scars from forming. And though it was tight and uncomfortable, especially when the weather was hot and humid, the suit helped relieve David's constant itching and stinging caused by the red, swollen flesh and scar tissue beneath it.

Early in September, David was testing at a second-grade level. Although he had always tested higher than his class, it was a sign he had improved radically. The surgery on his neck had been completed successfully. The hospital had done what it could, so we were ready to go home. David and I were both homesick. Brooklyn was only an hour away by air. Finally, we decided it was time to leave. We began to plan our journey home. Judy Curtis flew to Boston to help us. Ken Curtis and Officer Terry Branum flew to New York to help John arrange for our arrival. Somehow word got out that David was coming home, and the people of Brooklyn began to prepare their welcome.

We wheeled David quickly through the crowds at Logan Airport in Boston to the waiting Eastern Airlines jet. The captain himself greeted

David as we pushed him toward the plane. He invited the three of us to join him in the cockpit for a preflight tour. David was ecstatic. We lifted him from his wheelchair into the pilot's seat. He operated all the controls he could reach. He pushed the foot pedals enthusiastically. A reporter snapped pictures as David pretended to fly that jumbo jet. The next day we saw the pictures on the front page of the New York *Daily News*.

When we landed at New York's La Guardia Airport, great crowds of people and press from around the world were waiting to welcome David home. Remembering what had happened in Boston upon our arrival there, I was afraid to disembark, but Eastern Airlines and the New York police had an efficient welcome planned. The press were in a special waiting area. The crowd seemed well in control.

"Mrs. Rothenberg," a stewardess addressed me quietly upon our arrival at La Guardia, "we would like you and David to disembark first. There is a large crowd waiting to greet him."

The other passengers stood in the aisles, waiting patiently as the police prepared to guide us off the plane. I expected David to be wheeled from the airplane in a wheelchair.

But when the signal came, he refused to be wheeled or carried from the plane and began his long exhausting walk up the exit ramp.

Flashbulbs exploded like fireworks. Cameras whirred. Reporters spoke into microphones. It was like MacArthur landing at Inchon. In fact, David and the old general walked a lot alike. Shoulders hunched, eyes peering straight ahead, hands swinging, feet rocking back and forth on unsteady legs, David marched through the crowd without looking to the right or left. All he needed was the general's corncob pipe. Everyone watched my son wearing Reggie Jackson's baseball hat and his bright red and blue jogging suit. Some people cried. Other people cheered. Hundreds just watched in silent wonder as that determined little boy began his life again and refused to waste a moment getting started.

When David saw John and Ken and Terry Branum he smiled broadly. Media people were everywhere. In spite of the police and airport security, we were tripped and jostled, pushed and shoved. It was New Year's Day. It was the Fourth of July. It was Christmas. It was David whirling around in Ken's arms. It was me kissing John. It was Terry, Judy, Ken, David, and me climbing into a limousine and laughing and crying and talking like children all the way to Brooklyn.

David was in great pain. By the time we reached New York he was physically exhausted.

"Why did you walk, Davie?" John asked, impressed by the boy's accomplishment. "Last time I saw you in Boston, you couldn't walk at all."

"I didn't want people to think I was a baby," David answered and, for a moment, we all were hushed. Only a month ago, because of his injured brain, David had been reduced to infancy. For thirty days he had struggled to regain the use of his brain. He tried so hard to recapture the years he had lost when something went wrong in that operating room. He still wasn't able to control his bladder. He still slurred his speech from time to time. He still struggled to remember forgotten words. Had he known all along how important it was for him to win the battle against that swollen brain? Had he improved so quickly because he himself had determined it?

"I didn't want people to think I was a baby!" he said again, and we glanced back and forth at each other in the limo and wondered at his courage and determination.

Then we saw it. There was a mob flooding from the sidewalk in front of our apartment house out onto Court Street and into the Carroll Street Park. Almost one thousand neighbors had gathered to welcome David home. A banner two stories long hung from our third-floor apartment window. It glittered and shone in the light. Balloons flew from the fire escape and the iron fence. People cheered. The limousine passed slowly through the crowd. Thanks to John and Terry, dozens of policemen were on hand to control the happy mob.

We worked our way through the crowd and into our apartment house. One by one the police allowed news teams up the stairs to interview us and then escorted them down again. The next-door restaurant, Casa Rosa, opened its kitchens to feed the press and the police as well. David went immediately to his room and sat on the floor and began to play Atari with his cousins and his friends.

For a brief moment, I looked at the crowd smiling up at us. What drew them together? They came from middle-class homes in Brooklyn. Some were rich and educated. Others weren't. Some had regular jobs. Others were out of work. Every family faced crises of its own. Each person there suffered from his or her own tragedies and disappointments. What brought them from their homes and jobs, from their schools and playgrounds to stand in the sun and cheer a seven-year-old who had survived a murder attempt by his father? They didn't know

David. They didn't know me. We were strangers when we had left this neighborhood almost seven months ago. What were they cheering? Maybe it was just a wonderful surprise party for my son. But it seemed like something more. I looked across the room at David and his friends intent on playing David's Atari game.

Then I looked out the window at the people down below. Many eyes were filled with tears. A few handkerchiefs were raised and waving in old and tired hands. Just beyond the crowd in Carroll Park, I could see the statues of a soldier and a sailor standing in mute tribute to the boys from this neighborhood who never came home. Many of the people cheering my son were the fathers and mothers, the wives, children, and grandchildren of those same Americans who went off to war and never returned. Were they cheering David and thinking of their own sons, fathers, and lovers who were buried in the Argonne Forest or Iwo Jima, or El Alamein, or in unmarked graves somewhere? David might have been suffering still, but he was alive. I heard their voices from the street below. "Welcome home!" they cried. And the sparkling banner hanging on our apartment read, "You're a special kid, David! Glad to have you home." I joined my tears of grief and gratitude with the tears my neighbors cried.

15

All too soon the streets were empty of well-wishers. The welcome-home banner was taken down and rolled up and put away in the closet. The sun went down that shone so brightly on almost one thousand cheering neighbors. It was night again. With the night, reality dawned. All the wonderful help you get in a hospital suddenly disappears when you take your patient home. It only took one long night to discover that I was in big trouble.

David's brain had been damaged. He was not the same. And though we had encouragement from the doctors in Boston that his brain would function normally again one day, there was no doubt about the changes the accident had made. Those first nights home David still had no way to control his bladder. Understand: it isn't just getting up when he cries to change the sheets and pajamas. It means you must strip off his tight-fitting Jobst suit, bathe and treat the still raw and open wounds, re-cover his scarred body with lotion, pull on the three-piece Jobst suit again, resplint the child from head to foot, remake the bed, and hope it doesn't happen again before morning. It did, often.

Every stage of the night-long process caused David pain and increasing discomfort. His body was still weak and his emotions were fragile. His anger and his tears were all too near the surface. In his half-asleep, half-awake state he lashed out at me. It was bad enough to go through the many stages in changing my son and getting him ready for bed again, but to struggle against his angry resistance and to hear him cry real tears of pain unnerved and exhausted me.

Fortunately, Ken and Judy Curtis and Terry Branum were still with us. And the excitement of being home and being surrounded by old friends and family from New York and new friends from California got us through those first exhausting days. In spite of his ongoing struggle to recoup the losses caused by his swollen brain, David himself was also a constant source of joy and wonder to us all.

The day after our arrival, I saw him standing in his bedroom window looking down on Carroll Park and listening to the voices of the neighborhood children playing there. The day before we had held him up to that same window to wave to the cheering crowd. Now things were back to normal in Carroll Park. Old men played bocci ball and argued in loud Italian dialects. Women pushed baby carriages, gossiping and giggling as they strolled. A wild, rough-and-tumble football game was in process on the cement playing field. A large crowd had gathered to cheer and boo the two neighborhood teams. And miscellaneous children roller-skated, break-danced, and teeter-tottered in small, happy clusters about the park.

Our third-floor apartment was packed with well-wishers. We were eating leftover chicken and spaghetti from David's welcome-home party. Ken was reading aloud a story on David in the morning paper featuring a full-page headline, "Welcome Home, David." Others read through papers featuring stories about David that talked about "The Burn Boy Returns" and "Kid Courageous." Everybody was laughing and crying and remembering favorite David stories, but he was staring out his window at the park below.

"I want to go to the park," he said quietly.

That was no small request for David to make. His face was masked. His neck was collared and his arms were in splints. He wore a clavicle strap to keep his shoulders from contracting. His hands were small, round, and bandage-covered. When he walked, it was with great discomfort. To be held up before a welcome-home celebration is one thing, but to present yourself in person among your friends and neighbors close up for the first time after such a terrible burn was something else.

"I want to go to the park," he repeated quietly.

Of course, it was a natural request. We should have thought of it. But we didn't. Why? I suppose we were more afraid of people's close-up reaction to David's burns than he was. Besides, we thought he

would be exhausted from his journey and the excitement of his welcome home. But intuitively, he must have known that the gap between
him and the children on Carroll Street had to be crossed. David
wanted to waste no time in crossing it.

"I want to go to the park," he said again. And finally, we mobilized
to help him. He selected his new gray-and-turquoise sweat suit and a
pair of white tennis shoes with blue stars for the occasion. John carried
him down the steps and our apartment full of people emptied out onto
the street behind them. He had caught us by surprise again, and again,
it was hard to catch up with this daring and determined little boy.

After the stairs, David refused to be carried any farther. Ken walked
on one side, John and I on the other. His temporary day nurse scurried
along behind. David rocked back and forth as he shuffled across Court
Street and into Carroll Park. The people saw him coming and stopped
in their tracks. Bocci balls were ignored as old men stood quietly in
awe of the child who crossed the street in their direction. Mothers lifted
their children to see the sight. David looked straight ahead. He was
going somewhere and thirty or forty of us followed after him. He
walked right into the football game. Players screeched to a stop and
then both teams formed a moving V to get him through the crowd.

"Atta boy, David," a great big linebacker yelled across the field.
"You can do it!"

The players moved aside as my son walked right through them as if
they were not there. "Yea, David!" somebody cried. And others
around the park picked up the cheer.

"Go for it, kid!" a tough Brooklyn teenager encouraged from the
sidelines.

David didn't seem to hear them. He was going somewhere by the
shortest possible route. And the huge and curious crowd walked just
behind. Young people cheered, old people cried, and we hurried to
keep up.

"The kid has more guts than all of us," Ken whispered. "Most people scarred like David would have crawled into their rooms to hide."

People nodded in agreement, focusing on that little form in his Reggie Jackson baseball cap and jogging suit, waddling like a little turtle
across the park. His arms stuck out awkwardly from his sides. He
peered out of the slits in his face mask without looking to the right or
left. I was so excited I began to shout encouragement with everybody
else.

"That's my baby!" I yelled. "You can make it, Davie!" A reporter
from the *Los Angeles Times* heard me shouting, "Look at him. Doesn't

he look like a champion?" I don't remember exactly what I yelled that day but I remember exactly what I felt. I felt gratitude to God for refusing to answer my first prayers. In that first shock, I prayed that David would die. Now, months later, I was glad that he was alive. I was sorry he was scarred and suffering, but I was glad he hadn't died in room 139 of the Buena Park TraveLodge. God had blessed this kid and was using him that day to make us all glad for life, grateful for health, and confounded by the resilience of the human spirit that God had planted in each of us. "You can do it, Davie!" I yelled again and again, praying that he could and would continue to be able to face all the long and painful walks ahead.

Suddenly he stopped before an old teeter-totter. "I want to ride," he said. Finally, we knew his destination. He had always loved that see-saw and the swings and slides in the center of the park.

"So up you go," said John, lifting David onto the teeter-totter. Quickly another child was commandeered and placed on the other end of the seesaw. David was balanced in place by John and his nurse. Up and down they went. David didn't say a thing. With his mask, it was difficult to tell whether or not he was smiling.

"Did you like that?" someone asked as they lifted Davie down again.

"It was good," he whispered hoarsely.

"One day you'll be out here on your own again, riding your bike and everything," John promised my son.

"When?" David asked. "When?"

Immediately, David turned and began to walk back across the park. Again we all followed. Again both football teams made a V formation to get Davie through the crowds. Again the people cheered. As we approached Court Street, a team captain ran up to Davie and wedged a game ball into his arms. Davie didn't stop or even thank the teenager. He just hugged the football to his chest and walked on.

As we crossed the street in procession after him, Stella McHugh, the crossing guard for David's grade school, said, "I feel like I'm watching a smaller version of *Rocky* or something. God bless him."

Later that day in the apartment, we were celebrating David's victory. "There are going to be some tough times, too, Marie," Judy warned. And all of us shook our heads in agreement. "And where are you going to church?" she said without a pause. It was so natural for Judy and Ken to connect the "tough times" ahead with my need to find a church where David and I could worship. They took me aside during our few quiet moments together and encouraged me not to let one Sunday pass before I had found a church and made our presence known to the Christian brothers and sisters who attended there. They also prayed with David and me that God himself would help us through whatever lay ahead. I had no idea how badly I would need that advice and those loving prayers.

Just days after our arrival back in Brooklyn, a front-page headline in the New York *Daily News* neighborhood edition read, "New Hurdle for David: Some Oppose His Return to Class." It was true. I suppose I should have expected it and prepared myself for the shock, but I didn't. People had been so wonderful to David at UCI and at Shriners that I never saw or understood or estimated the power of the dark side of all that loving support. As long as David was a kind of celebrity who people could see and applaud at a distance, things were easy. It was the day-by-day, next-door, next-desk, look and touch that bothered a lot of people. Even some of those who cheered could not handle David close up.

The school system quickly provided David a home teacher who would be available to him five days a week. We were grateful. But Davie wanted to be back in school with his friends and if Davie wanted it, I wanted it, too. It would not be easy.

PS 58 had an active parent-teacher organization. Looking back, I have no anger about the small group of parents who had honest fears about David's return to the classroom. A meeting was held between school officials and those same parents who were concerned both for Davie and his classmates. In essence, they were asking, "Why should normal children be exposed to an abnormal child like David? Why should children be exposed to David's serious injuries? It might frighten or alarm those of primary-school age and even older. It might cause them nightmares. It might create questions that would be hard, if not impossible, to answer." Some angry words were said. Others spoke on David's behalf. "You'll soon discover," one of our neighbors told the group, "that David is a normal child. He may be encased in a badly damaged body, but the child inside is just like your child and mine. What has happened to Davie is not his fault. He should not be penalized for what his father has done. David needs PS 58," she said, "and PS 58 needs David." Apparently it was a long, hot meeting but cool heads prevailed and loving neighbors made the right choice. I was glad.

Of course, to the children, David's return to school was not an issue. "Davie, when are you coming back to school?" they would shout across the park at him. "Hi, Davie. We miss you," a little girl called up at Davie's window. Cards and letters bearing, "We love you, Davie," came from dozens of his former classmates and friends.

Soon after we returned from Boston, I heard our buzzer ring for the hundredth time.

"Who is it?" I questioned through the intercom, expecting another camera crew or newspaper reporter.

"It's Damien, Mrs. Rothenberg," he said. "Can I see David, please?"

"But Damien, we just got home, honey," I answered, trying to discourage him. I didn't know how Davie's old playmate would respond to his scars and injuries.

"Please let me come up," he insisted. "Davie's in my class. Remember?"

"Yes, I remember," I answered, "but don't you think—"

"Mrs. Rothenberg," he said, sounding a bit offended, "Davie and I are best friends. I want to see him now."

I pushed the button that unlocked the outside door. The sounds of a child's footsteps echoed up the stairway two steps at a time. He ran past me through the open door yelling, "Davie!" at the top of his lungs. David was standing looking out the window to the park. He only had time to turn before he found himself wrapped in the arms of a loving playmate. I stood in the doorway trembling a bit, watching fearfully.

"Davie, you're home!" Damien said. "What's that?"

"That's Robo-Man," David explained, haltingly, pointing at the new toy.

"How do you work it?" Damien asked, walking toward the toy and leaving David at the window. For a moment, David paused. He looked up at me. I wanted to help him walk those awkward steps to join his friend. I couldn't. David wouldn't have liked that. He shuffled slowly toward Damien, who was already kneeling beside the Robo-Man. David painfully lowered himself down beside his friend.

They played together most of the morning. Damien didn't ask about the deep scars or the missing fingers. He didn't even seem to notice the stiff arms and legs or the crippled walk. It was almost time for lunch when I talked to Damien again.

"Damien, I'm going to take David's mask off now," I started to explain. "He's going to have to eat. It isn't comfortable for him to eat with his mask on."

"That's okay," Damien said. "I don't care."

I watched carefully as I slowly pulled off Davie's mask. I revealed a seven-year-old child with no ears, almost no nose, and most of the features of his face burned away. David watched Damien carefully as I watched him. The boy didn't even seem to notice.

"Do you still play Pac-Man, Davie?" Damien asked, looking David straight in the eyes and smiling.

"Yes, I beat John last night," Davie answered hesitantly.

"Oh, good," said Damien. "When your lunch is over, let's play."

Then Damien reached across the barriers and hugged my little boy. David looked awkward and a bit embarrassed. He could not hug back. His braces held his arms out from his sides, but both Davie and I felt Damien's hug down deep inside us where hugs make all the difference.

Most of the children were wonderful, but there were adults and children who found it difficult to handle Davie's new look. Several days after our return I was passing his former day-care center when a woman who recognized me as a parent but not as David's parent struck up a conversation. "I think this lady is doing things far too fast, don't you?" I thought I'd caught her drift but I remained silent, curious and ready for a fight. "She's pushing that kid, don't you think? We're not ready for it. Why put the poor child in that position, where he will be exposed to stares and questions from all the other kids?"

I had been hearing those questions more and more since we arrived from Boston, and the poor unsuspecting lady got a dose of my pent-up frustration. "What do you expect me to do," I shouted, whirling to face her on the sidewalk, "hide my son in a closet because you don't want to look at him?"

Realizing her awful mistake, the poor woman was speechless.

"David has as much right to live in this society as you have," I continued, "maybe more. He has been through hell and now he deserves a chance to live a normal life again."

When she just stood there staring, I continued my attack.

"You people are narrow-minded and stupid to even suggest that my wonderful child be kept isolated from the other children. David will teach them as much about real life as all their classroom lessons put together."

"But what about his scars?" she muttered. "Isn't that going to be embarrassing for him?"

"David is learning to live with his scars," I answered more calmly now. "Would you let them separate him from the other boys and girls?"

"I'm just thinking about *him*," she said defensively. "Do you think he can handle it?"

"Don't worry about David," I said. "He has more guts than you will ever have in your lifetime. Worry about your own prejudice. That's what could keep him in the closet."

I'm afraid I was less than polite during those confrontations. I began to realize for the first time what it felt like to be a member of a minority. Brooklyn is a crazy, wonderful quiltwork of minorities, all patched together trying to make a whole where only parts exist. There are blacks and Latinos, Italians and Germans and Slovaks. There are old and young, rich and poor. There are straights and gays, healthy and handicapped. And David and I soon discovered what it meant to be a minority even to all the other minorities. We were cheered and applauded, but we were also stared at, ridiculed, pitied, and misunderstood.

Seeing David on television and in the newspapers so regularly made other people wonder if I wasn't exploiting my child for some kind of fame or fortune. That really made me angry. People can't understand how difficult it is for one to be pursued by camera crews and reporters and how difficult, if not impossible, it is without secretaries and bodyguards and powerful organizations to avoid the media and maintain any kind of privacy. We didn't ask for media attention. We never sought it. It has caused us great inconvenience and pressure and discomfort. At the same time, the media have opened many doors for David and for me. We have met new friends and had exciting new opportunities through our television, radio, and newspaper interviews. And a lot of money has been collected through the media to help pay David's bills.

It was impossible to care for David in his current state without nurses around the clock. At first I thought all my wonderful friends who volunteered to help us would make the difference. Angela Arrabito, for example, is one friend who worked almost nonstop to get us through those first long weeks. During my divorce from Charles five years before, Angela was also facing hard times. We shared our money and our food then. We rolled pennies together. And, years later, when David and I returned from Boston, Angela appeared again. Every day she helped bag the mountain of stained linen and pajamas, towels and bandages. Every day she took out bags of laundry and returned them clean and folded. There were other friends and family, too many to count, who did their best to help us. But I just couldn't do it with volunteers alone.

David needed a physiotherapist to visit each day to stretch and manipulate his muscles back into shape again. He needed an occupational therapist to reteach him basic motor skills. He needed special tutors to help renew his damaged brain. Every time we entered or left the apartment, there were three flights of stairs to carry David up or down. And often, I spent entire nights changing linen, pulling off body garments, washing, ironing, massaging, bandaging, redressing wounds, and resplinting limbs. I was exhausted most of the time. It was too much to handle on my own.

I called a nursing agency and got twenty-four-hour nursing help. It was not a luxury. In the hospital, it had taken whole teams of professionals to keep David squarely on the road to recovery. I was trying to do it alone. No wonder: the cost for nursing was close to five thousand dollars a week. Add to that the other costs: personnel and transportation, hospitalization, special doctors and surgeons, equipment, medicine, splints, and braces. Just keeping track of all the bills became a nightmare.

My insurance company faithfully paid the bills included in their policies on David, and the funds started by the Buena Park police met so many of David's other bills. Still they continued to flow in an endless and overwhelming avalanche.

But there were signs that David was regaining the mental and physical skills that he had lost. And that made all those overpriced and underexplained bills we were receiving worth the cost. For David was on the mend and there seemed to be a light at the end of the long, dark tunnel.

Children, like their adult counterparts, respond to David's injuries quite differently. Camille and Serina, for example, are two lovely neighborhood girls who are devoted to David. Serina plays games with him by the hour and Camille will even help David scratch the scars when they itch and burn him terribly.

The experiences with children range from cruel to hopeful. At a birthday party, a four-year-old girl approached David and asked him about his burns. For a moment she stared at him. Then she announced to the entire group of children, "I don't like David at all." At an amusement park, children will pass David and whisper loudly to their friends, "Yech. Did you see that little monster go by?" Some even point and shout cruel remarks from a distance. On the other hand, one four-year-old walked right up to David in Central Park. "What's wrong with your face?" she said.

"I was burned," David answered matter-of-factly.

Then she grabbed his arms and started to roll up his sleeve. "Were you burned on your arms, too?" she asked.

"Yes," he answered patiently, "all over."

"Everywhere?" she asked sympathetically.

"Yep," David answered, "everywhere."

For a moment the little child paused, then she reached her hand right into David's mouth and grabbed his tongue. "Well, you weren't burned on your tongue," she said very encouragingly. "You can be glad for that, can't you?"

David said, "Yes," and wasn't even bothered by the conversation.

In some ways, David's burns and the national publicity he received have given him some awesome advantages. Recently, he was invited by Merrill Lynch to visit the New York Stock Exchange. He was driven in a chauffeured limousine. He was led out onto the governor's platform on his tour. Suddenly the electronic ticker tape above the floor quit quoting market reports and read instead: "DAVID ROTHENBERG IS HERE. WELCOME HIM." Business on the Stock Exchange stopped. Brokers, runners, and analysts looked up at my little son and cheered him for a full minute.

He's been a guest of Marty Lyons of the New York Jets. Members of the New York Rangers hockey team visited him in our apartment and left him autographs, uniforms, hockey sticks, and pucks. New York's Mayor Koch sent Davie a wonderful letter welcoming him home and an "I Love New York" pin from Tiffany's. George Steinbrenner, owner of the New York Yankees, invited David to sit in his box on opening day. Vince Ferragamo of the Los Angeles Rams sent David a picture and letter saying, "I'm really pulling for you, David. I know you'll make it." And television star Erik Estrada sent a letter saying, "Be strong, get well, have faith." Many other athletes, professional teams, film and television personalities, and political figures wrote to encourage and inspire my son. And thousands of other people have written, sending cards and letters, presents and checks, in a national outpouring of love that David and I will never forget.

David's role in Brooklyn as a Carroll Gardens local celebrity continued as well. Team members from the neighborhood softball league asked my son to throw out the ball at the opening of their championship game in Carroll Park. It was quite an honor. Residents, especially the young people of our neighborhood, are sports addicts. Somehow David managed to give the ball a mighty toss and everyone cheered his effort.

Our new McDonald's restaurant in Flatbush Avenue Extension and DeKalb threw a special party for David and fifty of his old classmates and friends. Ronald McDonald was there making cards vanish, turning strips of paper into ribbon, and pulling endless handkerchiefs from his clown-suit pockets. The owner of that franchise met David just weeks before riding a float in the Atlantic Antic Parade.

There were endless celebrations and get-togethers like those. All of them prepared David and his friends for that moment when David would return to school again. The Shriners Burns Institute in Boston sent a three-member team to help David's classmates, teachers, parents, and school administrators prepare for his return. I had gone back to work to keep my health insurance that was vital to paying those ongoing bills, but I asked for the day off to be a part of that important briefing. I was not allowed to participate in its first stages. That made me angry. But apparently my presence could have inhibited honest questions that people wanted and needed to ask. A social worker, David's discharge nurse, and an educational consultant flew from the Shriners Hospital in Boston for that event. First they would meet with the principal of PS 58. Then they would brief the school's entire staff at a special luncheon meeting with the parent-teacher organization. Finally, they would meet with David's class.

"Why isn't David in special education?" one teacher asked. "He is a handicapped child now, after all. He needs special attention, doesn't he?"

"Until David was six, he had no handicaps," the specialists from Boston answered. "He needs to be treated as every child is treated."

"But what about the classroom problems he will have?" another asked. "At the present moment, we hear that he cannot even go to the toilet without assistance."

"Can he use a pen or pencil," someone else asked, "since his fingers have been amputated?"

"Can he participate in gym?" another wanted to know.

"What about the children? Will he cause problems for the other children?"

According to those who did attend the various briefings, the specialists answered each question patiently and convincingly. Most of the questions were asked because people were curious. No one wanted to keep David out of PS 58 if he could handle the daily tasks required there. Everyone at the school seemed willing to work a little harder to assist David when and how he needed it. The specialists were convinced that David could make it. And I was grateful for the Boston Shriners Hospital with what they accomplished in those important briefings.

The last stop on the day's briefing was David's third-grade classroom. They invited me into that briefing with Mrs. Hoerburger and her class. I sat in the back of the classroom as the social worker and the discharge nurse explained what had happened to my son and how it would affect him. They showed the students a Jobst garment like David wears. They explained why he needed splints. They talked about skin grafting and how it works. They told them why David needs to wear a mask and what the children would see behind the mask when he took it off in the cafeteria. They explained why temporarily David would need a nurse nearby. They were clear and kind and skillful.

The children's questions surprised us all. They took David's problem in stride. They were more concerned about David's father. "Is he in jail?" one child asked. "Could he escape?" asked another. "Is David safe now?" wondered a third. Obviously, David's classmates were ready and willing to accept him back as one of their own regardless of his problems or how he looked. What they could not stand was the idea that David might still be in danger, or that his father might try again to kill or harm their friend.

Something in the briefing that was said over and over by the briefing team made me angry.

"David will never look normal again," one social worker said repeatedly.

"What is normal?" I whispered to myself as I sat in the back of the room. "Who sets the standards for what *is* normal?" Were they saying that he will not have clear skin like everybody else? Did they mean that at least for a while his facial features will be partial, at best? What is normal? What is abnormal? The questions whirled in my brain.

I wished that I could have stood to say it another way. "When you first see David," I would have said, "you may be shocked and surprised at the changes the fire has made. In many ways he doesn't look like everybody else in the room. His head and face are different. His nose and ears, his mouth and eyes may seem strange to you. That's all right. They seem strange to David, too. But don't let that worry you. Gradually a miracle will happen. David will begin to look normal again. Soon you won't even notice the differences because you will see that the little boy who wears that face is still David and David is normal no matter how his burned face is changed. Once you know the person behind the face, once you've laughed and talked and cried with that person, you will start forgetting the 'abnormal' features. Soon, you won't even notice the differences. You will know David and because David is beautiful, thoughtful, and creative, soon his face will be as beautiful to you as the child inside that face. So though he may look 'abnormal' to you at first, just wait—soon he will look normal again."

To tell the children that David would not look normal again might make it true. It wasn't true at all. It happened to the doctors and to the nurses. It happened to friends and family. It happened to me. At first I was shocked and sad to see what happened to little David, but by staying with him, talking to him, playing with him, something wonderful happened. Time passed, and David started looking normal again.

But I didn't need to worry. The children already knew that.

"David," I said on that first day, "Your nurse is here. It's time to go."

"I know, Mom," he answered, ready for that reentry into third grade.

I don't know why I stalled that morning. I suppose every mother fears how other children might react to her own precious offspring, but David was already through the door and trying to grip the banister of the three-story stairway to lower himself to the street below. He stepped onto the sidewalk and already children were gathering to walk Davie to his class. "Hi, Dave," a classmate said. "Can I carry your books?"

"Morning, David," another said cheerfully. "Glad you're finally coming back." Again, David looked straight ahead. He didn't speak. He only nodded as he shuffled toward the corner.

"Good morning, David," said Mrs. McHugh, the crossing guard. "Have a wonderful day."

It *was* a wonderful day. My son was alive. He was walking on his own two feet. He may walk with a stiff, side-to-side roll; his arms may stick out a bit, but he was walking. Up the stairs he went and down the hall and into his classroom. The students saw him coming. The minute he rounded the corner and entered the class, the children began to applaud. Suddenly, David stopped. He turned around and walked back outside the classroom once again. The children looked back and forth, confused. The teacher wondered what had happened. Finally the class stopped applauding. Then, and only then, did David turn to reenter the classroom and join his friends.

16

Early in November, David and I returned to the Shriners Burns Institute for his first major outpatient checkup. He was examined by a whirlwind of doctors and nurses who undressed him, inspected his grafts and amputations, ran him through an assembly line of tests at breakneck speed, then called me in for consultation.

"Mrs. Rothenberg," the physiotherapist began, looking over a summary report of David's condition, "we have good news."

"Really?" I asked, surprised and pleased at his announcement.

"Yes, really," he affirmed. "David is doing so well we feel that he doesn't need his arm splints, his neck brace, or even his face mask anymore."

"You're kidding," I said, already anticipating how David would cheer that good news and the relief of daily pressure we both could celebrate.

"Take them off," he said with certainty.

"But I disagree," I responded, surprising even myself with the words. It isn't easy to disagree with a person in authority. I was scared and he was surprised.

"No reason to disagree," he said. "The splints and the mask can go."

"Are you sure?" I asked again.

"Yes, of course," he answered. "David just doesn't need them anymore."

Again I earned my reputation as the most cantankerous mother of the year. Three times I asked if he were sure and three times he answered yes without hesitation. I was puzzled. I had been teasing, begging, forcing, loving, and jamming David into his forearm and hand splints, and his neck collar, every day and night for nine months. I knew what happened the moment I allowed him to con me out of them with his tears or threats or promises. His arms contracted almost immediately. To see his little forearms and hands pull inward toward his chest could break your heart. Those awkward and often painful splints were the only way I knew to keep it from happening. Yet in a quick once-over exam, the authorities determined that the splints were no longer necessary.

We returned to Brooklyn and for three days I left David's braces and collar off as the physiotherapist had instructed. And, in three days, David's hands contracted considerably. Without his neck collar scar bands began to form on his neck, leaving it stiff and awkward. At the end of three days, I went back to the old plan and decided to return to California to visit Dr. Achauer and our friends at the UCI Burn Center.

I write this story not to disparage in any way the Burns Institute or its people. Doctors and nurses around the country recommend that Boston hospital as one of the great burn-treatment centers in the world, and I am sure it is true. But even a great burn center can make a mistake. Those same mistakes might have been made by Dr. Achauer and his colleagues at UCI. The point is that parents or family or close friends who work with the patient day and night must constantly review the decisions of the authorities and make decisions of their own.

I didn't trust anybody with my son. I remained the advocate and the adversary of the authorities. I used my eyes to watch his healing process on my own. I used my brain to decide whether a treatment was working or not, and I stood and fought against decisions I felt might be harmful to David's healing. Those were scary, self-doubting times, but after nine months nursing my son full time, I began to trust my insight and intuition as much as I trusted anybody else's. To most doctors and nurses, a patient is only one statistic in the lineup during one more crowded, pressured, stressful day. But to a parent, that particular patient must be the only one in the line who matters. I believe the patient's parent is responsible to supervise and evaluate the medical profession at every stage along the way. It isn't easy, but it can help guarantee a child's healing and might even save his life.

In December I returned with David to the UCI Burn Center in California. Dr. Achauer and his team seemed genuinely glad to see me. In spite of my constant questions and confrontations, my tears and my often angry and intemperate words, Dr. Achauer would listen. He would let me have my say. He was willing to look the long distance into David's future and plan accordingly. He didn't keep secrets, even if the news was painful or alarming. He tried to explain to me everything that was done at every step along the way. He let me help him decide when the issues were complex and the chances fifty-fifty. He made me a member of his team. I wasn't the parent forced to bide my time, helpless and alone, through scary days and lonely nights in waiting rooms and hospital cafeterias. I was encouraged to be an active part of David's healing. They trained me to work with my son. They let me make my own mistakes. They corrected and complimented me as I questioned and complimented them.

Dr. Achauer made David a part of his treatment team as well. The doctor assured me that as my son grew older, he would have opinions of his own as to what reconstructive surgery he himself valued more important or more urgent than another. David's opinions, too, would be considered all along the way. To the UCI burn team, David was another person, a little seven-year-old person, true, but a person with feelings and dreams and ideas of his own.

We learned of one young teenage burn victim at UCI who had serious disfiguring facial and body burns. He was ashamed and embarrassed by his appearance and tried to hide himself from friends and family. Reconstructive surgeries were being planned. He desperately needed facial reconstruction and surgery on hands and feet as well. Dr. Achauer's team and the boy's parents included him in the important decision of what reconstructive surgery should be done next. Everyone agreed that rebuilding the outer ear was one of the last surgeries necessary—that is, everyone but the burned boy himself. He wanted his ears rebuilt first. When they asked him why, he said, "More than anything I want to get a short haircut like my friends but I can't without ears." They decided to meet the child's request and almost immediately after his ears were reconstructed and his hair cut to style, the boy became outgoing and gregarious again.

That's the long-term view. That's considering the patient's opinion as important as the authority's or the parent's opinion. That's learning to listen and to rearrange priorities when the listening is done. That's why we went back to California.

A burned child is treated in three different stages. The first stage is resuscitation—just trying to save the child's life. Walking inside the

UCI Burn Center the day we returned, I was almost overcome by memories of those first weeks when David fought for life. I walked past the hydro room and remembered my suffering child lowered into that bath, where folds of dead skin burned black by the flames were sloughed away. I remembered watching him fight off the deadly bacterial infections. I remembered them trying to force the oxygen tube down his tightly constricted throat when David stopped breathing and turned blue. But we had survived those days, David and I. Visiting UCI with all its painful memories was, for me, like visiting my son's empty tomb.

The second stage of treatment for a burned child is rehabilitation. That stage lasts from six weeks to six months. Again memories flashed and danced. I saw David pushed, unconscious, from the operating room with his little hands stretched up into the air, pins forced through the base of each finger, and most of his fingers cut off, the stumps still swathed in bloody bandages. I remembered his feet cut away and bleeding. I remembered those screaming sessions when Bob, David's occupational therapist, forced my son's arms and legs back into the proper place for splints.

Rehabilitation had hilarious memories as well. I remembered David refusing to catch the therapist's beach ball, then finally hitting a painful home run that bounced off the therapist's head. "Like Reggie," David chortled. And I remembered that little bead necklace strung by a child with no fingers and held up to me with pride and dignity.

Now we were at UCI to continue our third stage of treatment—the reconstructive stage. Dr. Achauer took David's arms in his hand and ran his fingers down David's healing scars.

"They are healing beautifully," he said. "And look at that beautiful job the surgeon in Boston did on your neck."

"I itch all the time," David interrupted.

"And the itching is awful," Dr. Achauer commiserated, "but you have to itch, David, for a while. It's another sign of healing, but you won't have to itch forever, I promise."

Dr. Achauer explained that a scar is a fibrous tissue which is the body's glue. Anytime you have an open area, the body forms a scar tissue to cover and protect it. "We can't grow new limbs like reptiles or regenerate new parts," he said. "All our body can do is lay down scar tissue to heal itself. As they mature, the scars get red and thick. They itch painfully. They're tight and miserable. Jobst's pressure garments keep scars growing flat like normal skin. The Jobst suit and the anti-itch medicine will help control your itching, David, but they cannot stop it altogether. During this time, the scars like to contract," he continued. "Scar tissue pulls tightly, causing the body to tuck inward." Dr. Achauer and the therapist used physiotherapy and splints to help David avoid permanent contractions. However, sometimes, as in Davie's neck tuck, surgery was required to release the neck. "But David, your scars will soon be white and soft and beautiful," Dr. Achauer assured him in conclusion. "Now we want to give you hands again."

On Christmas Eve day, December 24, 1983, ten months after the tragic fire, David got his long-delayed visit to Disneyland. Officials of the Magic Kingdom gave him the kind of red-carpet treatment normally reserved for visiting dignitaries and heads of state. I watched hundreds of visitors, who had read David's story in their newspapers or seen our interviews on network television, stand in silent admiration as David met Mickey and Minnie Mouse on the steps of Disneyland's City Hall. David was wearing a California Angels baseball cap that Reggie Jackson had given him and a new Mickey Mouse watch presented by Disneyland's Ambassador to the World. People grinned and waved and applauded as David and our little parade of Southern California friends were guided through the Magic Kingdom.

David rode every ride that day, but his whispered instructions to our guide guaranteed that the first adventure in Fantasyland would be a visit to "It's a Small World." We rode together through the colorful waterway with mechanical dolls representing the children of the world singing, "It's a world of laughter, a world of tears. . . ." I couldn't help but think how many of those boys and girls in real life are victims of child abuse and how little anyone is doing to protect them from physical and emotional injury and death.

David didn't say much to the reporters and the crowd of spectators who gathered around him that day, but he did comment softly, "It was the best Christmas I have ever had." On the front page of the *Los Angeles Times* Christmas Eve edition, one Disney executive was quoted as saying, "We've had visits by kings, emperors and other dignitaries, but David is someone special. He just tugs at your heart."

That same Christmas Eve we went back to Eastside Christian Church, where I had made my decision to become a Christian and to be baptized. Memories stirred as I walked through the door. People from Judy's Bible class rushed to greet us. A great Christmas tree was decorated in the entryway. The church was ablaze with candles.

Dozens of people I remembered gratefully hugged us and welcomed us home.

We walked slowly to the front of the church and sat together in a pew near the choir. It was a Christmas Eve candlelight service and everyone was singing Christmas carols: "Joy to the World," the people sang, and tears ran down my cheeks and spilled over into my lap. "The Lord is come." It was true. For though there were many times I didn't feel His presence in surgery waiting rooms or in the Holiday Inn, He had been there in spite of all my feelings. He had loved David and me through these, His singing people. They had caught His joy and they had shared it with us. "Repeat the sounding joy," they sang. "Repeat, repeat the sounding joy."

David sat unmoved by my tears, glad to be sitting with his friends again. He held onto Kenny's hand and watched the people sing. Then the organ began to play the first quiet notes of "Silent Night." Suddenly David came to life. He remembered that carol and grabbed the hymnbook out of my hand and started singing, "Silent night, holy night. All is calm, all is bright." He sang loudly. I mean he sang *so* loudly that the people all around us turned and listened to that rather squeaky, high-pitched voice: "Round yon virgin, mother and child, Holy infant so tender and mild." His facial scars were red and tight but he had live and growing skin again. His lips and ears and most of his nose were still gone but soon they, too, would be replaced. His lungs poisoned and scarred black by the fire had healed themselves so he could sing. His fingers were gone but he balanced the hymnbook on the top of his tightly contracted hands that Dr. Achauer promised would soon work almost naturally again. "Sleep in heavenly peace, Sleep in heavenly peace."

Since that first day in the intensive-care unit at UCI when I met Ken and Judy Curtis, they, their family, and their Christian friends had prayed for a miracle in David's life. But what had God actually done in answer to their prayers and mine?

I could thank Him for the courageous strangers who burst into David's burning motel room and dragged him from the flames. I could thank Him for the quick-thinking paramedics who worked to stabilize David's condition even as they rushed my charred and dying child to the Burn Center. I could thank Him for the doctors, the nurses, the therapists, the counselors, and the administrators at UCI and the Shriners Burns Institute in Boston for the skills they used and continued to use in resuscitating, reconstructing, and rehabilitating my son.

Those are certainly gifts for which it is appropriate to thank God.

But what did Ken and Judy's prayers have to do with the exercise of those natural gifts? Where was the miracle in this child the media was calling "The Miracle Boy"?

Isn't a miracle an event so unexplainable to man or woman that we have no other choice but to call it an act of God? The acts of heroes, paramedics, doctors, nurses, physiotherapists, and counselors can all be explained. Even the body's healing, certainly a gift from God, has been scientifically analyzed so that it is no longer a mystery or unexplainable. So where was the mystery? Where was the miracle in David's life that Ken and Judy prayed for?

As we sang in the Christmas Eve candlelight service, I realized that Ken and Judy Curtis, their family, and our new Christian friends were themselves the miracle that they prayed for. For as I looked back on this yearlong nightmare, the one thing I couldn't explain was why Ken and Judy and all the others loved us so. What they did for us day after day in Jesus' name was the real miracle. We can explain all the rest.

David and I flew to California in January for David's next corrective surgery. When he was safely out of danger, I returned to my job in New York, leaving David in the hands of the Curtises. He loved living in that warm, happy family environment. He especially liked going to basketball games with Melanie at Whittier Christian High School. The cheerleaders practiced in the Curtis backyard. He sat on their laps and learned every cheer. He loved the attention his waving arms and raspy voice would bring.

Late at night Melanie and Greg would say their evening prayers with David. They told me how he prayed for me and for Charles and for his friends. Then before he closed his prayer, David would yell out a Whittier Christian High School cheer: "W C H S, W C H S, Fight! Fight! Fight! Amen."

David loved to pray. The Eastside Christian Church had a prayer garden on the grounds. On his first visit to the colorful flower garden, Greg and David sat on the prayer bench and prayed. "Lord, bless my mommy and my daddy," David began. "He did a bad thing. Help him not to do it again. And help my mommy to want to move to California. W C H S, W C H S, Fight! Fight! Fight! Amen."

The next morning I called to see how David was doing. During the conversation, I mentioned casually that I was thinking of moving to California to be nearer to UCI and the Curtises. That was all it took to convince David that God really does hear and answer prayers.

Prayer is so much a part of Ken and Judy's life. I don't think a night went by when David stayed with the Curtises that Ken and Judy didn't stand beside my sleeping child, place their hands on his head, and pray for God's loving will in his young life. One day Judy confessed that she was secretly praying for hair to grow back on David's head. His hair follicles had been burned away and there was little chance of his having natural hair again. A few strands of hair had survived the fire on the left side of David's face. One morning Judy whispered, "You know, I counted two new hairs on the top of his little bald head today." There's a verse in the Bible that God knows every hair on our heads and has them numbered. Judy was helping God keep count of David's.

Greg Curtis is a college sophmore. While doctors were trying to save David's life, Greg and his friends began to visit my son regularly. The visits were real productions. The kids are hams. In fact, Greg's friend Dave Avenzino made extra money doing singing telegrams around Southern California. On the first visit, Greg's friend played young David, who grew up to be king of Israel. Greg came as Goliath. Complete with pretend slingshot and wads of paper for stones, they acted out that ancient confrontation between little David and the giant. Greg, hit in the forehead with a wad of paper, crashed to the hospital floor, groaning dramatically. My David cheered as the Bible's David won the victory. They always finished that favorite play with a reminder that God loved the ancient David so much that when Jesus was born He was called the son of David and that God loved my David just as much.

These young Christian kids did more in their visits to resurrect the spirits of my son than any medical or psychological treatment could have accomplished. Both Greg and Dave were performers. Often they would perform David's favorite songs for him. Above all of them he liked the theme song from the television series "The Greatest American Hero." "Believe it or not," they would sing, "I'm walking on air, I never thought I could feel so free. Flying away on a wing and a prayer, Who could it be, Believe it or not, it's just me."

During their first visits, David was masked and swollen. He had a tube from the respirator inserted down his throat. He couldn't sing or speak but he laughed with delight as they sang. "S-s-s-s-s" was all the noise his laughter made, but it lit up the room. As Greg left after the first visit, he leaned down and whispered to David. "Do you know who Jesus is?" "S-s-s," my son whispered, nodding affirmatively. "Do you know that He loves you very much?" "S-s-s," my son replied again. "I'm going to ask Him to make you better," Greg promised. Visit by visit, David did get better. During his last stay with the Curtises as an outpatient at UCI, David had been listening to songs recorded especially for him by the children's choir of Robert Schuller's Crystal Cathedral. They sang songs from Scripture and substituted David's name in every verse.

Little by little, my son began to understand the nature of the Christian faith. In fact, we learned the basics together, he and I, and we are still both learning. One afternoon, during our last visit to Ken and Judy's, David stumbled onto a book featuring pictures from Franco Zeffirelli's television special "Jesus of Nazareth." Greg had the colorful and graphic book in his room. David loved seeing the pictures and hearing the story of Jesus, but when Melanie turned to the pictures of the Crucifixion, David gasped. "They killed Him?" he said, shocked. After all Ken and Judy, Greg and Melanie, and their friends had been telling him about Jesus, David couldn't believe that somebody would kill such a wonderful person. "Sometimes people hurt other people and don't even know themselves why they do it," Melanie said.

"I know," David answered softly.

"But look what happened." Melanie turned the page to reveal a full-color picture of an empty tomb. "He didn't die for long. God brought Him back to life."

"Oh, no," David said, unbelieving, "how could that be?" Again, Melanie tried to explain. It wasn't easy. How does one tell a bright seven-year-old boy that there are no satisfactory answers for the really difficult questions, only faith.

One night in his bedroom, David was listening to a song called "The Family of Jesus." When Judy entered his room to say good night, David said quietly, "The family of Jesus must be really, really big."

"Yes, it is," Judy replied, tucking him in. "And I'm in it."

"You are?" David asked, sliding beneath the covers. "Is Bubba in it, too?" he questioned, using Greg's nickname.

"Yes, he is," she said.

"And Ken and Melanie?"

"Yes. All of us," she answered, sitting down on the edge of David's bed.

"What about my mom?" he wondered. "Is she in the family of Jesus?"

"Your mom is a Christian, too," Judy said.

"I thought my mom was an American," David corrected.

At that point, Judy stopped to explain how simple it is to become a member of that family. She told him about my decision and about my baptism at the church. "You see," she concluded, "your mom is an American but she also knows Jesus."

"Well, I don't know Him," David said slowly.

"Well, you can, you know," Judy continued. "It's so easy."

"I want to know Him, too," David said matter-of-factly. "I want to be in His family."

"Well, just ask Him."

Later Judy told me that David bowed his head and asked Jesus to come into his heart in a clear and simple prayer. When he finished, he looked up at Judy and said, "Is Jesus inside me now?"

"Oh, yes, David, and He will never leave you, ever," she said.

"Is He in my hands and my toes?" David asked.

"Yes," she said, "in every part of you."

"Will He make me well by morning?"

Judy stopped for a moment, she told me, thinking hard about that one. Then she spoke again. "From the moment you were born," she said, "Jesus was there helping you. He loved you before you were burned and after. And He will go on loving you forever."

"But will He make me well tonight?" David asked.

"Jesus doesn't work that way, Davie," Judy explained. "He will be with you every step of the way and He will heal your body. But He will heal it slowly, as the body is supposed to heal."

"What about my scars?" David asked.

"You may have scars for a long, long time, maybe forever. But Jesus will help those scars heal, too. And one day, a long time from now, you'll look back and you will know that He has been in you, loving you, helping you, and healing you all the time."

For weeks, David would tap his chest with his hand and say to people, "I know Jesus. He lives in me. Right here." And then he would sing, "Believe it or not, I'm walking on air, I never thought I could feel so free. Flying away on a wing and a prayer, Who could it be, Believe it or not, it's just me."

I can't explain exactly why faith in God has been so important during our time of crisis. I just know what a difference it made for David and for me when Ken and Judy Curtis shared their faith in Christ with us. The Christian community, too, has overwhelmed us with their love and their support. We could not have gotten along without them.

This loving support helps because I still alternate between faith and doubt. I still have trouble forgiving Charles. And both David and I occasionally wonder if we will survive those nightly battles, fighting to get him bathed, his open sores medicated, his body rubbed with cream, his head massaged with beeswax, his Jobst suit pulled on, and his braces laced in place. Sometimes the hours-long process is almost overwhelming to the both of us. We fight and yell and ask forgiveness, but we are learning and we are growing slowly.

David has been remarkably courageous in the face of his tragedy. During his stay with Ken and Judy, he insisted on being taken to room 139 of the Buena Park TraveLodge, where he almost died. One of his favorite nurses, Dee Fraser, accompanied by Judy and Ken and the police to the motel.

"He never really explained why he wanted to go back so badly," Dee told me on the telephone. "He said it was just something he had to do."

When they arrived at the motel room, David recognized the site immediately. He began to tremble when they entered the room and he began to breathe rapidly as they stood around the new bed. But David seemed glad to see that everything had been repaired and to hear again that no one else had been hurt in the fire. And he didn't seem over-whelmed or terrified by the experience. On the ride back to the Curtis home, when asked how he felt about the visit, David said simply, "I feel sad. I feel very sad." Somehow word got out that David wanted to face his father in prison. Responding to that courageous wish, hundreds of abused and sexually molested children have written David sharing their own cruel experiences. Many of the letters we have kept from him because they were so poignant and so tragic.

Several parents have written whose children have disappeared or have been murdered. They write to encourage us. "Even though David may be scarred," they write, "he is alive. How much we wish we have our children back, in any condition, rather than gone forever."

I don't know about the future. Ken and Judy, Greg and Melanie, and our new friends in Southern California go on amazing us with their Christian love. And day by day we grow more hopeful that God can take our tragedy and turn it into something meaningful for David, for me, and even for Charles.

Now I'm looking down from our third-floor window at David on the sidewalk below. He's walking with his nurse to PS 58 today. A few painful minutes ago he slammed the apartment door with all the strength a seven year-old could muster. I stared at the same door, choking down my own anger and tiredness just long enough to hear him wrap both arms around the wooden railing and begin the long descent to Court Street three flights below. And I crossed the living room, picking up an armload of plastic splints, medicine bottles, and ace bandages that still littered last night's field of battle. Now, leaning against the bookshelf and staring out through the frost-framed window, I watch him walk his stiff, determined shuffle through the brown-stained icy slush that covers Carroll Gardens.

Halfway down the street, he stops and turns his face toward the window where he knows I'll be waiting. He is less than four feet tall. He is breathing little puffs of steam as he stands looking up at me. His grafted arms still arch slightly from his body. He looks lost in the oversized Mickey Mouse jacket he received at Disneyland. And the Angels hat from Reggie Jackson is pulled far too low over Davie's head and ears. He looks round and vulnerable and magnificently determined.

Slowly he lifts his stiff left arm in a half-wave, half-salute and, just as slowly, I wave back. His burn mask covers almost all of his face except those dark brown eyes. And even from this distance, his wonderful eyes signal up to me that all is well between us. All is forgiven. We have survived one more night of healing. It is a long and tedious road we travel together, but we are getting there. Thank God!

"Have a good day, David my son. I love you very, very much."